Magick *for* Transformation

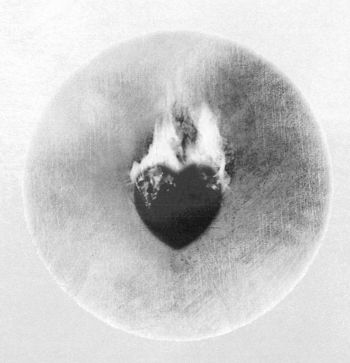

Magick *for* Transformation

Rituals and alchemy for manifesting your wildest dreams

Brandi Amara Skyy

CICO BOOKS

LONDON NEW YORK

To all those ready to believe in magick. Nothing is impossible, and you/i/we/us are the wild souls who will manifest it ALL into being. Go forth and be proof of what is possible. And so it is.

Published in 2024 by CICO Books
An imprint of Ryland Peters & Small Ltd

20–21 Jockey's Fields   341 E 116th St
London WC1R 4BW   New York, NY 10029

www.rylandpeters.com

10 9 8 7 6 5 4 3 2 1

Text © Brandi Amara Skyy 2024
Design and illustration © CICO Books 2024
For additional picture credits, see page 144

A CIP catalog record for this book is available from the Library of Congress and the British Library.

ISBN: 978-1-80065-374-0

Printed in China

Editor: Kristy Richardson
Designer: Geoff Borin
Art director: Sally Powell
Creative director: Leslie Harrington
Head of production: Patricia Harrington
Publishing manager: Carmel Edmonds

Contents

Foreword

Magic is our birthright. Every one of us comes from magic, is connected to magic, and is magic here on the Earth, our home. Magic is at the crux, the core of everything. It is the roots of the old and ancient tree.

I could end this foreword with this reminder but I won't, because I have a few things to share with you. As an author, writer, and Witch, it's an honor to be here with you, peering through the pages of this book, celebrating its existence and presence in the world, and offering a few thoughts. Thank you, Brandi.

Brandi has always impressed me with her genius insights, sparks of inspiration, and ways of thinking outside the box with all she creates. She is a teacher, a guide, a liminal walker, and a magic maker. Her stories and retellings are lanterns in the shadows. They will help you see yourself through.

I first met Brandi through the Witch Wide Web, a community connecting through the threads and in the corners of the internet. We bonded over Word Witchery, the act of writing as ritual, and stories. There is Word Witchery at work in these pages. Early on you'll find the quote "Words are wands." The words in this book shape themselves into an intention—a way to wield not solely power but empowerment through the pages.

This book is a guide. So, I'm here to ask you, "What you will do with this birth right? This magic? The transformation that is waiting?"

The poet Mary Ruefle once shared that every word carries a secret: its etymology. I love etymology and one of its fun secrets is held in the word "mundane." It comes from the Latin *mundus*, which means world, a translation of the Greek *kosmos*, or "the physical universe." The mundane is connected to the cosmos. I dream of this as I fold my laundry, walk the dog, pay my bills, wash the dishes, and brew tea. I am mundane. I am magic.

When we remember our magic (if we've forgotten it) or celebrate our magic, it's truly a miracle what can (and will) unfold. This book reminds us of that magic and offers us portals—to connect with and deeply honor that magic, to honor our past selves, and to dream the biggest dream. It is an altar to be returned to again and again. Throughout the book, you'll find explorations, rituals, and invitations to deepen this magic and develop and craft your praxis (more on that later).

So before you begin, I would like to leave an offering at this altar as well ... an invitation: wherever you are reading this, right now, put your ear to the Earth, cast your eyes out the window, take a moment, take a breath, hear the birds, see the clouds roll past, and feel the tree bark with your palm. However you honor the world, however you take it in, I invite you to do that. Paying attention is a ritual, an act of presence. We are here on this Earth right now, perhaps the only planet in the entire universe with oak trees, dogs, the smell of soup cooking on a stove, and ancestors. As you read this, there may be new or full moons, astrological transits, seasons passing and changing, memories, intentions, releases, and celebrations. I invite you to pay attention to it all, ritualize it all. When you're living in the mundane, remember your magic and how it is inherent, as is your wholeness. You are the Earth and the cosmos.

I learned a lesson from snakes, who teach that right before they shed their skin, they go blind or their vision becomes fuzzy. Sometimes, we cannot see what is on the other side at the moment of transformation, but the blessings are waiting and sight will return. All things are in cycles, as they say.

This book tells us everything is possible until we believe it isn't. And this simple thought alone is a form of alchemy.

And so, what does it mean to truly transform using magic, nonetheless? The etymology of alchemy is perhaps from Khemia (an old name for Egypt), literally "land of black earth" or from the Greek *khymatos*, "that which is poured out." Be of the Earth. Pour it all out. Transform, again and again. See where the paths wind, what stories you bring with you, and what new stories are forged by the experience. Here's to your magic, all your past and future selves, and the possibilities and portals. I'll see you out there.

Kate Belew
Writer, poet, storyteller, and Word Witch, co-host of podcast Magick & Alchemy, and co-author of *Wild Medicine: An Illustrated Guide to the Magick of Herbs.*

INTRODUCTION:
Porta

Openings. Portals. Vortexes of possibilities.

On the following pages, you find yourself in front of them all, in the place where everything begins.

Every card, every word, every choice is an archway, a doorway, a gateway.

A return pathway back

To the ultimate kernel of truth.

You are the Sacred Creatrix of your life.

All things grow and flow through you.

It's time to remember.

It is time to begin.

Origins of a Wild Dream Witch

i was five years old when i fell in love with the night sky and all the legendary tales, archetypes, and ology that are hidden behind its blinking, midnight veil. i wished so hard for magick, that we finally found each other in the form of constellations, Milky Ways, comets, and stars. Astronomy and astrology became my first self-discovered forms of magick.

Growing up, i wanted the kind of magick i watched *Cinderella's* Fairy Godmother weave, that turned pumpkins into carriages, ragged clothing into couture, and bare feet into glass slippers. When it came time to clean my room, i wished for the wand-weaving spells of *The Sorcerer's Apprentice* that brought brooms, buckets, and washcloths to life to do all the cleaning. (Spoiler alert: i still do.) i wished for Schmendrick's (albeit clumsy) magick to turn myself into a unicorn and back again; Snow White's ability to call forth and speak to forest animals, and Mildred Hubble's admittance into Miss Cackle's Academy for Witches, so i could learn to be a witch and marry Tim Curry.

A Magickal Childhood

Unbeknownst to me, i had been surrounded by magick since birth. My grandmother, Mommo B, was well-versed in plant medicine and the remedies of our people's ancient *curandera* (Mexica Indigenous healer). i lived vicariously through my father's stories about my grandmother's healing magick, how she would forage medicine from bushes and trees in the backyard for whatever ailment he felt; i clung to his tales about the full-body egg sweep she would perform before he went to bed; how she would leave the egg under his bed until morning, then crack it open to reveal the all-black yolk and liquid inside.

i gained access to my cultural magick in other places, too. i found it in St. Patrick's Roman Catholic Church, among its pantheon of saints, in the stations of the cross emblazoned in the stained-glass windows, in its Frankincense-filled air, in the ritualized movements and moments of the service, and in the prayers, rosaries, and candles i would be instructed to light in penance.

i felt mi gente's magick—the magick of my people—in my grandma Gloria's food, in my mother's healing hands, and in my father's stories. But most importantly, i was beginning to sense and find it within myself.

Finding My Personal Alchemy

The year 2020 was a time that changed all of us. But as the entire world locked down during the COVID pandemic, my little universe collapsed. Simon, my four-legged, 14-year-old companion, was dying. He transitioned from physical protector to spirit guide on the morning of June 1, 2020 and i turned to magick to console me. When i picked up my tarot deck the morning after Simon's death and received the exact card and message from Spirit i needed, magick became something so much more.

i began to build a different relationship with magick, one that was deeply personal and metamorphic. The continuous choice i made that day changed my life. Magick became a pathway to healing, a modality of support, a forever relationship that encouraged me to evolve. It became a porta (a gate or doorway) to radical personal transformation—what i call, Radical Personal Alchemy, which is the bones of this book. It unveiled worlds, words, visions, archetypes, and opened up new ways of feeling, sensing, being, and living with myself and life. It ushered in the reclamation of my Indigenous ancestral lineage of medicine and magick, my company Woke Magick (a coven of Sacred Creatrixes), a field of Wild Dreams, and a wonderland of me.

My Magickal Praxis

Before we shift our focus from magick to transformation, i want to (briefly) share the style of magick i practice. It is the basis of everything—from journal prompts to spells to invocations to word selection—in this tome. The kind of magick i teach and practice in my orbit is:

Non-denominational: It doesn't subscribe to any magick tradition's dogma, and you don't need to have any magickal lineage affiliation to practice it.

Radically intersectional: It is the magick of and in the nepantla (the in between spaces). My magick is liminal, a place where all things meet and then become something else, a sacred third, or even fourth, fifth, or more. It is an energy all unto its own.

Intersectional Alchemy: Intersectional Alchemy is a collective term for all the modalities, energies, and intersections my magickal praxis touches.

My personal Intersectional Alchemy sits at the crossroads of two worlds: my Indigenous ancestry and my chosen Western Occult one. From this crux, it welcomes sacred connections of other modalities like astrology and tarot and invites modern-day practices and real-time of-this-world experiences into the conversation and fold. You'll learn all the specifics about Intersectional Alchemy later in the book (see page 93).

The two forms of magick that my personal Intersectional Alchemy is mainly based on are the Aztec Medicine Wheel and the Seven Hermetic Principles. These two principles inform, support, influence, and amplify one another.

The magick of the Aztec Medicine Wheel and all its natural correspondences is drawn from my Indigenous ancestry. The Wheel is based on the four directions, the elements, seasonal cycles, and animal allies, but it also brings in specific Aztec deities, colors, and periods of life. We will dive deeper into the Aztec Medicine Wheel later in this book (see page 98).

The base, legs, and foundation my magick rests, intersects, and dances upon are the Seven Hermetic Principles, which are sometimes called the Seven Natural Laws of the Universe. These principles, along with the *Kybalion*, the Emerald Tablet, and other traditional Western Occult texts, guide how i live my life and what i do, create, and conjure with my magick.

Together, these two pillars, the Aztec Medicine Wheel and the Seven Hermetic Principles, make up my spirituality and practice—and form the foundation of everything in this book.

Find Your Own Transformational Porta

As a Capricorn Sun, i have a burning need to make esoteric things tangible, to make airy ideas manifest in the three-dimensional world. To take what i have learned and shape it into something understandable, usable, and transformational for others. And perhaps, more importantly, for that transformation to be in service for the highest good of all involved—ourselves included.

Because what is the purpose of radical transformation if all we do is go back to living our regularly scheduled lives? No, mi gente. Your past is not your future if you make different choices in the present.

In this book, i pass on everything i've learned to you, so that you may break free from your hooks and tethers, and steward in your miraculousness, so that you too can live your Wild Dreams—those brazen dreams about writing a book, starting a business, or quitting your day job to travel the world—those dreams that others told you were impossible.

Because here's what the naysayers' reality won't allow them to see—anything is possible until you believe it isn't. You/i/we/us are living among the miracles—internet, electric stoves, 9.58-second 100-meter sprints, blood transfusions, iPhones, flight—that were once deemed impossible by oh so many. You were once an improbable 1-in-a-million impossibility. And yet, here you are on the precipice of becoming even more of what you already are—magick. You've already beaten the odds. You're already a miracle.

The only thing new i'm showing you in this book is how to claim it, how to alchemize your experiences via magick, and then transmute all of it into a tool to support your becoming, now. Here's to your metamorphosis.

*May you, your life, and your creations be undeniable
proof of what is possible.*

*May the shares in this book be a gateway to your own
brilliance and a steward of your medicine and magick.*

*May the transformations you seek find and bind to
you, forever.*

May you always know your own agency and power.

*And may you always weld it in sacred service
to the highest good of all involved.*

And so it is.

Thank you. Thank you. Thank you.

Before We Dive In

There are a few notas that need to be spelled, weaved, and broken before we leave our introduction for the depths of transformation.

Words Are Wands

As you navigate through these pages, you'll come across some peculiar spelling and capitalization. This is all intentional and on purpose and you can find the terms "magick," "i," and "praxis" explained in greater depth in the Glossary (see page 140). It's imperative for me to empower the work, words, and my people's voices and medicine in this book. It is all part of my special brew and blend of magick.

Protection and Boundaries

Do i believe in *mal de ojo* (the evil eye)? Yes. Do i believe we—not only as magicians but as spirits having a humxn experience as well—need to protect ourselves and protect our magick? Yes. Do i believe we need to cast circles to do so? No. Casting circles is not my lineage of magick. However, if casting a circle feels most true for you, heed that.

Always remember that boundaries—between you and your work, your body and your spells, and the energy that is yours to carry and the energy that is not—are always required. When it comes to protection and boundaries, trust your instincts and intuition to recognize what you need and then put that into practice. Please practice magick safely.

Cultural Appropriation

Cultural appropriation is defined as taking elements and rituals from specific cultures, using them out of context, and acting as if you own them with no regard or respect to the peoples and lineages that they came from.

i believe that ALL magick comes from and is rooted in the same source (see the Seven Hermetic Principles, page 80) and from this source, all cultures felt into a path that was most true for them. Their specific needs cultivated a tradition of magick that was uniquely reflective of their time, situation, circumstances, and immediate needs.

Today, many of us are not privy to our full lineage of ancestry, especially if we are historically marginalized. Thus we, like our ancestors, must feel and fumble to find our way back to our magickal home. It is not my role to take that process of discovery away from you. i feel that we could all give ourselves and each other some grace because we are all trying to find our way. My responsibility is to remind you that there's an energetic difference between reverence and entitlement, respect and bypassing, and curious observer and malicious conqueror. Your magick knows the difference and will respond accordingly. And YOU have a responsibility to know the difference and act accordingly too.

Useful Tools

All magick is consensual. Or, at least, i believe it should be. There must be consent between you and the tools you work with, whether that's a tarot deck, pendulum, candles, or whatever. i believe in asking every one of my tools if they want to be a part of a certain practice or theme (like this book for example). i want you to get into the habit of practicing rituals of consent in your everyday and magickal life.

There are a few tools that will be useful to have handy at the onset of our journey, such as a tarot or oracle deck of your choice—one deck that you have an intimate, deep, and long-standing relationship with is much more powerful than a deck straight out of its box. Keep a candle solely devoted to this book, to be lit whenever you feel called, and also a notebook or journal. Choose your tools intuitively. And pay close attention to anything that pops or jumps out at you—it means they want to be part of your journey too! Ensure the journal is one that you are intuitively attracted to—it will become your grimoire (see page 89) and a tool we will work with later in the book.

i invite you to use what you have and resist the urge to go out and buy something new. Part of the medicine and magick we will be working with throughout this book is sustainability—for Earth, each other, and ourselves by learning to continue to choose the things we already have that once were "had to haves."

Four of Pentacles

Every adventure i go on—whether it's writing a book, coaching a flient (friend + client), or creating a course—always begins with me and my tarot deck, asking for a card as an energetic guide for the journey. The card i received as this tome's guide was the Four of Pentacles. In all honesty, i was surprised. A card that traditionally represents selfishness, possessiveness, and the hoarding of wealth? A miser showing up as the guide for a book about being open to the possibility? It didn't make logical sense.

Then i remembered how much i really love the illustration of this card from the Rider-Waite-Smith tarot deck. The character's direct eye contact somehow manages to emanate from the two-dimensional card and pierce the reader's soul. The cyclical frame of their arms around the coin, protecting their heart, reminds me to release my grip, let go, and trust in the highest good. As the only Minor Arcana figure to wear a crown, the Four of Pentacles alerts me to this truth:

That i always remain sovereign, safe, and sacred even when i lay my weapons down and open myself up to the transformation that being vulnerable brings. This is the energy that i'm hoping this book will unlock in you.

The Four of Pentacles offers a clear choice: Free yourself from the chair or stay there. The only thing that keeps you clinging and grasping to old coins, old comforts, old chairs, and all the old versions of you … is you. May you feel the joy of release that letting go brings.

PRAXIS: YOUR GUIDING CARD

Before you read on, take a moment to pull your own guiding card for the journey ahead. May you be held. May you be supported. May you find within the pages, words, letters, and all the spaces in between the courage to finally be all that you came here to be, experience, and express.

1 Shuffle your tarot deck. As you do so, ask for a card that will guide you on your transformational journey.

2 Select a card from the pack. The card you have chosen will become Card #1 (you'll learn more about this when we reach the end of Section 0, see page 46). For now, write it down so you can remember it.

3 Take a moment to fully land here, in gratitude, right where we are. As i type and you read, we open the space and prepare to venture on this journey together.

4 Take an inhale, breathing all our selves back into our bodies, back into our cells. Exhale in the white space between sentences, releasing all that will not serve you on your quest for transformation.

Invocation of Woke Magick

Are you ready for big, bold changes but you don't know where to begin, how to proceed, or which way to go? Whatever path you were on before, all are welcome here.

All trepidation, nerves, and skepticism are okay. i want to invite you to lay down all the weapons you use to guard yourself and relinquish the tight grip of the coin in front of your chest. Allow yourself to carry the medicine of past lessons with you but not let them define the path that lays ahead you. Because wherever you once found yourself, you are no longer there. You are here with me right now on the precipice of radical transformation. Now, let's begin.

PRAXIS: INVOCATION RITUAL

i invite you to go outside and taste the air on your tongue, feel the Earth solid beneath you, hear the whispers of guidance from the seasons, catch the scent of change dancing in your nostrils, see into your future, and sense the magick that always surrounds you. This is magick. This is what you came for.

1 With this book in your hand, step outside and face the direction that calls out most to you.

2 Stand (if standing is accessible to you) and/or straighten your spine, centering your chest over your belly.

3 Take three deep breaths. With each breath, allow every sensation and sound to seep in and every doubt or disbelief to be expelled out. Take it all in.

4 When you feel ready, open your eyes and in your full power read aloud the Invocation of Woke Magick (opposite).

5 Take a few moments to soak in all the energy of your opening ceremony. You just did real magick. Take. It. All. In.

6 When you feel complete, bow your head in reverence and gratitude, head back inside, and turn the page.

We, the collective, in divine union and highest good intent, call in the transformative medicine of the Wheel of Life.

We call on our ancestors and allies from all realms to be present with us as we take our first steps onto the Medicine Path in right relationship with Spirit, the traditional custodians of the land we reside on, and the guardians of real magick. Some of us as new venturers. Some as old.

Some as once lost now returning home.

We welcome you in. Please guide us. Please show us the way.

We call all shades, versions, avatars, shadows, pieces, fragments of ourselves, our souls back here. Back home. Back into our bodies. Back into our light.

And life.

We call our Medicine, Wild Witch, Priestess, Brujx, Highest selves fully here.

To be present on this journey regardless of where we are at in our lives or who we are with.

We are ready to welcome, embody, and praxis our Sacred Sovereignty.

May we carry and channel your messages and medicine through our magick and the art of our lives.

May we journey round the path forever unfractured.

Forever in harmony. Forever unbound.

Forever in solidarity to the highest good of all involved; ready to be evolved.

We are all magick here.

And so it is.

Thank you. Thank you. Thank you.

PART 0:

You Are Here

And so you begin. On the following pages, we call
in from the Aztec Medicine Wheel (see page 98) the
element of Air, the medicine of Mictlāmpa (North),
and their animal ally of courage, Black Jaguar. They
will help to sharpen your mind, cleanse, and protect
you as you lean into magick in metamorphic ways,
enter new Wild Dream landscapes, and discover
how you can transform your life once and for all.

And so it is. So shall it be. Thank you. Thank you.
Thank you.

The Foundations of Magick and Wild Dream Work

There is an electric chaos, like wild bolts of excited energy, that run through our body when we know we are about to embark on an adventure that has the potential to change the course of our life. Here you are, ready to jump off a cliff, and leap into a new arcana of your life. But what is it exactly you are falling into? How will you know if you have landed? When will you leave The Fool's void for the resources on The Magician's table?

0 THE FOOL

When i pulled my first tarot card the morning after my beloved animal kin, Simon, died (see page 11), i had no idea i was stumbling upon a relationship with magick that would forever change my life.

i was searching for solace, a reprieve from the heartache, anything to ease the ferocious avalanche of pain i was feeling. As i continued to sit at the same table morning after morning, returning to the ritual of pulling a card day after day, a natural shift began to take place. Anguish gave way to pain. Pain gave way to a deep desire to express myself and an even deeper desire for my pain to be of greater service. Eventually with space, time, and magick, Simon's death gave birth to Healing the Loss of a Pet, a tiny book about big loss (see Resources, page 141).

Through that experience, of transforming grief and loss into art, i taught myself the art of alchemy. Of transmuting pain into soul gold, and that gold into something tangible, that could also help others. i allowed the magick of my daily card to transform me into the creatrix, magick maker, and witch i had always wanted to be. Magick was helping me heal, grow, become, and evolve. It was helping me transform grief

and loss into art. And teaching me through experience all the things i pass onto you now.

But what exactly is magick? What exactly do i mean by transformation? How does it all work together? And how can magick and transformation help us reach our goals, live a life of miracles, and catch our Wild Dreams? We'll dive into all those answers now.

What Is Magick?

As a kid, i saw magick as something outside of me, something that happened with the flick of a wand, a quality that you are either born with or not. It took me decades to unlearn societal tropes and beliefs about what constitutes magick.

i realized that magick is not inherently or solely Wiccan, European, or white-centric. Magick is something i could gift, be, or learn myself. And so can you. Because magick isn't about semantics. It's about energy. And magick can (and does!) look like you. Magick can be many things (see page 26) but here's the main thing it's not: Magick is not passive.

Magick IS agency—a key to your personal agency as well as a link to all your power. Whatever brings you to magick—searching for the love of your life, opening the road for your next adventure, or attracting abundance—at its essence, magick is about reclaiming your power. ALL your power. Your power of intention, of decision, of focus, of action, of will, of sovereignty, of your word, and, most importantly, your power of self ... the place where all magick begins.

MAGICK IS ...

Magick is the thing(s) we cannot quite get a grip on or wrap our heads around.

Magick is elusive. Secretive. Quiet.

Magick is bold. Loud. A firecracker detonating the fates of our life.

Magick is the force that animates all life.

Magick is the art of creation—and destruction.

Magick is relationships—to yourself, your tools, Spirit, Divine, the cosmos, us, all, and everything.

Magick is a spell, a wish, a hope, an impossible dream come true.

Magick is the creative impulse, the yearning for expression, and the art that is made from it.

Magick is energy and intent made manifest through spiritual will.

Magick is medicine. And medicine is magick.

Magick is infinite—with no beginning, middle, or end.

Magick is everything and all.

Magick is your birthright.

Magick is your will made flesh.

Magick is the pulse behind everything that makes you, you.

Magick can harm, hunt, and haunt you. But it can also free you in ways you never knew you were bound.

Magick and the Self

Your Self—as in your body, consciousness, mind, heart, and everything in between—is the entry point to magick. Your Self sets the magick and the actualizing of it. The power of and behind your spells, the force and motivation of your actions, and the dedication and determination with which you live your life, are all sourced by you.

Because magick is self-sourced, it is only as potent, focused, and strong as you are. How you treat, speak, and tend to yourself is directly proportional to the impact your magick and actions will have in manifesting the things—and life—that you want.

Your Self is so important in magickal work that i've devoted the entire first section of this book to helping you learn and embody the skills that will help stretch and strengthen your sense, belief, behaviors, and energy of your Self.

For now, i want you to get a clear picture of where you are at the beginning of this journey. To begin your exploration, start with the following journal prompts:

- How different is my life right now from where i want it to be? What do i feel is missing? What are the key differences?

- How much do i trust myself to do what i say i'm going to do? To finish what i start? To stay committed for the long haul? To do what needs to be done?

- What do i feel has kept me from experiencing the breadth of my magick power? What stories do i tell myself about power? What do i believe about power? What do i believe about my magick?

After reading this chapter, complete the self-assessment at the end of it (see page 45). We'll return to your answers at the end of our journey so that by the time you reach the end of this book, you can truly witness how much your Self has grown and changed.

What Is Transformation?

Transformation is both an art and skill. Like art, some kinds of transformation are unteachable—it happens all on its own accord. Other kinds of transformation happen through our power of choice. This kind of transformation is a teachable skill and is the kind of transformation will be working within this book.

Transformation is magick—the same, alchemical process that changes base metals to gold. It will transmute your experiences and emotions into Soul Gold. The transformation you'll undergo throughout this book comes in a variety of shades. Some transformations will be immediate, dramatic, and drastic. Some will be quiet, subtle, and unnoticeable—at least at first. The goal in transformation isn't to become someone completely different, that would mean that everything about us now isn't good enough and nothing could be further from the truth.

Transformation of Choice

Transformation of choice is consciously choosing to put oneself through a specific transformation. i invoke my power of choice by choosing to do drag (see opposite), a choice that unlocked a whole new world of transformations that would not have been possible or accessible to me if i had not made that initial choice to participate in it.

You, too, made a choice to buy and implement this book. It has opened a Pandora's Box of ideas, teachings, and magick that you might not have known before or come across outside of it. By choosing this book, you've actively invited transformation into your life. This is a powerful thing.

Choosing to be an active participant in your transformation is a powerful thing. Choosing to transform in the first place is a powerful thing. Choosing to do something different or

A STORY OF TRANSFORMATION OF CHOICE

To transform into the enigmatic persona of the Brandi Amara Skyy that hits the stage, i begin by looking in the mirror and really seeing my face. i take in the naked visage staring back at me, and look at all the slopes, lines, and textures of the canvas i have to work with. i hit play on my iPhone, and as the opening notes of the song i'm about to perform drifts into the chorus, i breathe in tonight's wish: that the energy, the show, the expression i'm about to drag out onstage will transfix the audience and make them feel something—entertained, awed, transformed.

i know, from all these decades of doing drag, that the real transformation begins right here—in the desire to be more, the moment of choice, and in the action of picking up my brushes to paint my face.

Every stroke of clown white, every whisp of eye pigment, every eyelash, rhinestone, overdrawn eyebrow and lip is a spell that casts me deeper into the betwixt and between of who i was and who i'm consciously metamorphosizing into being. A spell of half here and half there. Of AFAB to Queen. Of mundane to magickal.

out of your comfort zone is a powerful thing.
And being in your power is what magick is all about.

Now, i want you to reclaim and proclaim your own transformation of choice by powerfully saying these sentences out loud three times:

"i choose transformation. i choose to transform.

And so it is.

And so it shall be."

Preparing to Transform

It's important for you to build a personal relationship with transformation and the way we do that is by swimming in the ocean of our why. On the following pages, i'll help you get even more clear on your why and how you can use this energy in service to your goals, Wild Dreams, and wishes.

We aren't transforming just for transformation's sake, we are doing this because we want to feel, create, and/or BE something. What is it that you are willing yourself into being? In the next two chapters, Preparing for Your Journey and Your Magickal Tools for Transformation, i will teach you all nine of the magickal skills and nine magickal tools. i will show you how to use them in service to living into who and what you are becoming.

As much as i wish i could wave a magick wand and make everything you want from your life happen, alas, i do not hold that kind of power—but you do. Set yourself up for success by taking a quick inventory of your life, what's gotten you where you are now, and what needs to change to land you where you want to grow.

The final chapter of this book, Transforming Your Life, is devoted to helping you cultivate these answers. This chapter includes a 30 Days of Magick For Transformation challenge, which is intended to help you solidify your commitment to your highest self and your Wild Dream Life by guiding you through 30 days of living and praxising all the elements of this book.

The following praxis will help prepare your nervous system, heart, and mind for the content that lies ahead. It will also help you start to create your own relationship with the upcoming chapters and will be a beautiful place to return to see how much you've grown.

PRAXIS: TRANSFORMATION

Grab your journal and a pen. Go through each of the following prompts, taking care to feel into your answers and any other questions that might come up for you as you explore the terrain of you. Take your time with this. Let it be as long (or as short) as it wants to be.

1 In your journal consider the following prompts:

- Why do YOU want to transform?
- What were the things that brought you here?
- Why is transformation so important to you?
- What is your metamorphosis in service to?

2 In your journal consider the following prompts:

- Where do YOU want to go/grow?
- What and/or who is it that you want to transform into?
- If transformation, like magick, begins with us, where do you ultimately want to end up?
- Who do you want and see yourself being at the end of this cycle's magickal journey of transformation?

Take a moment now to reflect on your answers.

3 In your journal consider the following prompts:

- What will YOU commit to doing (or stop doing) to get there?
- What are some of the things you can start doing now? Or stop doing?
- How committed are you to yourself and this process?
- Do you trust yourself enough to finish what you started? How can you trust yourself more?

Take some time to write down all the things you are committed to doing and not doing.

Magick, Transformation, and You

Magick for transformation teaches us the most important lesson of magick: That before we attempt to do magick on or for others, we must first and foremost learn how to weld our will and power on ourselves. Because there is nothing more powerful than a soul lit up by itself.

Magick for transformation is a bridge to our whole, holistic self—a bridge between our lives and the archetype(s) we are magicking ourselves into being. Like a mirror, magick for transformation shows us what we are truly capable of—and what is blocking us from getting there. It requires us to raise our standards and then rise to meet them. It's about stocking your personal magickal toolkit with tools that you know work for you and help you build the kind of life, work, business, or art you've always felt was possible but never really knew how. It's about consciously working with these tools of magick in service to your personal growth, development, and evolution, and to remain congruent with your values, beliefs, and dreams while on the road to becoming who you were always meant to be. Magick for transformation is magick in service to your highest purpose and expression. Magick for transformation is the evolution of our planet that all begins and ends with you/i/we/us.

Transformation is big stuff. But it's also the tiny, subtle stuff. Magick for transformation is for folxs who are ready to make deep, lasting, forever, monumental change. That's the spell that is woven throughout the words in this book. And the magick this book will help you unearth and return to in yourself. Let it all in. Take it all in. You are on the right path. You've chosen transformation. Now it's time to invite magick in.

PRAXIS: YOUR ARCHETYPE CARD

One of my favorite magickal tools to help steward transformation is tarot. We'll be diving into how tarot can assist and amplify our transformation later (see page 115), but for now i want to invite you to grab your journal and a tarot or oracle deck that you are familiar with. It's important that you can identify the energy and/or archetype of each of the cards.

1 Get your body into a comfortable position and hold your deck in your hands.

2 Think about all the reasons you picked up this book. What were you hoping it would activate in you? What or who were you hoping this book could help you become? Think about the energy and frequency you want to call in.

3 Hold your answers in your mind as you thumb through the deck with the cards facing you.

4 Consciously and intuitively pick a card with the archetype and energy you want more of, or that you want to transform yourself into.

5 Now, set a timer for 10 minutes and journal about why you chose this card. Here are a few prompts if you need some guidance to get you started:

- What was it about this card and archetype that made you choose it?
- What energy does it emanate that you are hoping to cultivate in yourself?
- How does this card make you feel?
- What would a day in the life of this card look like?
- What message does this card have for you?

6 Just as you did with Card #1 (see page 19), write it down so you can remember it. The card you chose will become Card #2 and you will continue to build a relationship with these cards as you progress through the book.

Wild Dreams and You

i believe your dreams are the most important thing on Earth. They are the sacred callings of your soul that you came to this Earth to do. Your Wild Dreams can move mountains (and you!) to do any and everything you desire to create, be, and do.

When you pair your magick with your transformation and point the result toward the pursuit of your Wild Dreams, you pave the way for miracles to happen. You open the door for the divine to work on your behalf. Let's create a pathway for the miraculous, by rediscovering and remembering how to dream, wildly.

MY WILD DREAM STORY

In the mid-80s and early 90s, i was obsessed with ice skating. Aged nine, i had made up my mind. i was going to be an Olympic iceskating champion like my sheroes Oksana Baiul, Tonya Harding (pre-Nancygate), Surya Bonaly, and Rosalynn Sumners. There was only one problem. i lived in one of the hottest, most humid, and least iceskating-rink friendly city in Tejas.

But that minor detail didn't stop me from dreaming wildly about it. i opted for the next best thing—rollerskates! Every day i laced up my skates and taught myself the spins, small jumps, turns, and artistic footwork on our concrete backyard patio. When i wasn't in my skates, i dreamed up the choreography for skating routines to my favorite songs.

My parents took me to Cityskates, our local roller rink, where i performed my routines and everything else i had worked on at home. One day, in the middle of the rink, was a group of about five skaters. They were clad in classic uniforms, doing the exact same kinds of spins and jumps i saw on TV! So, i laced up my skates and joined them.

Once the professional skaters left the floor, i stayed in the center doing my self-taught skating choreography. But i noticed a man, arms tightly crossed, face tense, in a serious conversation with my parents. i immediately thought i was in trouble for joining the professional skater's and interrupting their practice. But he was actually the coach of the Cityskates Artistic Rollerskating Team—a group of skaters who did everything my favorite ice skaters did … but on rollerskates! And he wanted me to audition!

That was the day i inadvertently began a lifelong love affair with Wild Dreams. That one choice—to plant myself in the middle of the team and show off my skills, however wobbly and amateur they were—transformed my life for the next three years. In my time as an artistic rollerskater, i competed in over 10 competitions all over Tejas, two Nationals in Pensacola, Florida, and would go on to win 1st place in the Junior Olympics—just like 16-year-old Oksana Baiul did in the 1994 Winter Olympics. It laid the groundwork for a life full of chasing and catching my Wild Dreams.

What Are Wild Dreams?

Wild Dreams make up your very own, personal Wonderland. They defy logic, the system, the norm, and expectations. They are the dreams that muggle folxs (the status quo) label "impossible" or "pipe dreams"—too out there, too ambitious, and too crazy to actually come true.

Wild Dreams expose the limiting thoughts, patterns, and beliefs of those who proclaim them impossible. They challenge us to think, act, and live outside of traditionally accepted boxes. To achieve them would defy the odds and radically challenge what the collective consciousness believes is possible. Wild Dreams are magick—and by accomplishing them, you prove to the world that magick is real.

Most importantly, and contrary to what anyone else says, Wild Dreams are achievable. Wild Dreams are doable. By me, we, us, and YOU.

When i first entered Mētztli Wolf's Revolutionary Mystic World via Instagram, i was inspired by their unwavering commitment to their Wild Dream of opening a wolf sanctuary. Everything they discussed, shared, posted, and created in their online store was in service to that greater calling—and to their community. Then, right when their life seemed to be hitting a stride, it all came crashing down. They were forced to move from their house, and it appeared that their wolf dream would never happen. But they turned to their community for assistance and their community powerfully showed up for them—and continues to do so. Now, almost two years later, Mētztli has beaten a debilitating illness, opened the Black Moon Wolfdog Sanctuary as a nonprofit, and has rescued eight wolf dogs and counting. They are changing the world by showing other Black, Queer, Indigenous, and Neurodivergent witches and dreamers the power of collective care and having an impassioned mission.

Mētztli and i are just two Wild Dream catchers. There are WAY MORE WILD DREAMERS WINNING than we know. i hope our stories stretch and expand your mental muscles and belief in what is possible. There is no difference between these folxs and you. They used the resources they had—belief, hope, and community—to foster and create the magick that would then lead them to the transformation they sought. And their wildest dreams achieved! You have that exact same power.

i want you to make it your personal mission to find even more examples of people doing impossible things and living their wildest dreams. And then, i want YOU to become your own Wild Dream story for folxs like you to use as their proof.

YOUR WILD DREAM LIFE IS ...

Your Wild Dream Life is a life that you haven't even dared to dream of yet.

Your Wild Dream Life is a life in hyper-color, hyperdrive, and hyper-happiness.

Your Wild Dream Life exceeds all expectations, parameters, and limits.

Your Wild Dream Life is so fabulous that it will inspire others to dream wildly—and win.

Your Wild Dream Life will expand you beyond what you thought you were capable of.

Your Wild Dream Life will push you to be more, love more, and do more—not out of necessity, but out of pure passion for life. Your life.

Your Wild Dream Life is so scrumptious and delicious everyone will want a piece of it. But only those you want in will get in.

Your Wild Dream Life is the culmination of your Wildest Dreams come true.

Your Wild Dream Life boils down to how you/i/we/us live our life each and every day.

Before We Begin to Dream

If the idea of dreaming bigly, wildly, and so freely feels crunchy or uncomfortable, i want you to know that you are not alone. We feel comfortable with what we've been taught and led to believe is possible. Dreaming beyond our comfort zone is, in and of itself, a wild idea. This is big work for us folxs who have not had the privilege or opportunity to experience safe spaces that support— let alone literally buy into—our dreams.

If you need solid proof that you can do this (and even if you don't), grab your journal, and make a "proof list." This is a list of all the hard things you've already done. Everything counts— from leaving an abusive relationship to quitting smoking, from coming out as queer to starting a business—it all counts. All i ask is that you begin where you are, with what you have.

PRAXIS: **MY PROOF LIST**

The more you practice dreaming past your edges, the more and more comfortable you'll be stretching—and then moving—beyond them.

1 At the top of a fresh page in your journal, write the words, "My Proof List."

2 Set a timer for 15 to 30 minutes.

3 Go to town listing out all the hard things you've already done or been through in life. Take this slow or fast, the speed is up to you.

4 When your timer goes off, reread what you wrote and bask in the awe of all the amazing, hard, improbable things you've already done.

5 Type up this list and print it off. And keep it hanging some place you can see it every time you sit down to work, write, create, or magick.

PRAXIS: YOUR WILD DREAM ALLY

Know and trust that you are held, supported, and believed in. By your ancestors, by the other souls reading this book, and especially by me. We will explore ancestors and allies later in the book (see page 110) but for now, grab your tarot or oracle deck and ask for a Wild Dream ally that will become a beacon of support.

1 Find a comfortable position for your body and hold your deck in your hands. Think about your Wild Dreams and the energy and frequency you want to call in to achieve them.

2 Shuffle the deck and choose a card. As you look at the card, remember it is an ally that you can carry with you alongside you for the duration of this chapter, this book, and the rest of your life.

3 Write the name of your ally in your journal. Listen for any messages, signals, symbols, or sensations your ally wants to share with you and jot them down too.

4 Speak out loud this talisman in the form of a mantra: "i will not let anyone else's limits or beliefs dictate what i can and cannot do." Remember, the only real limit is you.

5 Just as you did with Card #1 (see page 19) and Card #2 (see page 33), write it down so you can remember it. The card you chose will become Card #3 and you will continue to build a relationship with these cards as you progress through the book.

As American author Glennon Doyle says, "We can do hard things" (see Resources, page 141). And as i always like to say, "We've already DONE hard things." Much, much harder things. Hold on to that truth as you dive—or just dip your toe—into the watery world of Wild Dreams.

Remembering How to Dream Wildly

To get to a place where you can dream as BIG and WILD as you know you're meant to, we first need to remember exactly what your Wild Dreams are—which is exactly where we are going to begin. Now we're going to turn impossibilities' mirror on YOU.

Your Wild Dreams are your why—the thing that keeps you going and growing through the curve balls of life. Your Wild Dreams are your anchor and your destination—anchoring you in the work you need to do to achieve them and becoming the source of inspiration you need to continue on the journey when the waters get rough. Your Wild Dreams can be anything—big or small, local or global, monetary or vocational, mundane or magick, and every and all shade in between. Your Wild Dreams might be to …

- Quit your day job.
- Start a business.
- Write a book.
- Move across the country.
- Buy your land back.
- Become a professional witch.
- Be the first at something.
- Get a record deal.
- Become a poet.
- Be a drag queen.
- Become a parent.

The only thing that truly matters when it comes to Wild Dreams is that whatever you are dreaming is yours. Your Wild Dream must be something you dream for yourself, not because someone else—parents, friends, society, tradition, culture—has dictated it for you. And that YOU believe in YOUR ability to succeed. That kind of belief has altered the course of the world. And that kind of belief will change your life.

The next praxis (see page 42) is a special gift to you because it is indeed quite powerful. i want you to come into this praxis empowered and like you are about to conduct a

powerful ritual for yourself—because you are. Latch your attention onto every single nuance, second, inkling, or intuitive hit you have; everything that comes up in this energy is information.

Whatever you write down, whatever your Wild Dreams are, none of them are too big, grand, or too far-fetched to achieve. And through the encouragement, praxis, and embodiment of magick for transformation, you'll be well on your way to manifesting them true.

PRAXIS: INDEX CARD OF WILD DREAMS

Freewriting is a form of writing where you keep your hand moving (see Tools, page 120). To try it out, gather your journal and a pen and something to time yourself with. You will also need index cards, preferably the larger 5 x 8in (127 x 203mm) size, but again, please use what you have. Grab a cup of your favorite beverage, which will be a supportive ally as you move through this spell. Sip, contemplate with, and enjoy it. Give yourself as much time as you can for this praxis as it will influence everything else.

1 Set a timer for 10 to 20 minutes.

2 In your journal, free write your thoughts on the following prompts.
- What did you dream about becoming as a child?
- What dreams, desires, or wants did others tell you were impossible?
- What dreams have you labeled impossible?
- If impossibility was suspended and any/everything in the world was possible for you, what would you dream for yourself? In other words, what impossible things would you dare to dream?

3 When you're done, give yourself some space from what you just wrote down. Go outside. Refill your drink. Step away from your desk or wherever you set up. Shimmy and shake out your body. The goal here is to shift your energy.

4 When you feel like your energy is reset, return to your journal, and re-read what you wrote.

5 As you read, pay close attention to bodily sensations, intuitive hits, or other synchronicities. What are the things that light you up, and that make you feel good as you read them? If something strikes you, rewrite those Wild Dreams, ideas, or sentences on a fresh sheet of paper. If you don't feel anything, that's okay too! When you're done, you should have a fresh and more condensed version in a list form.

6 Now from that list, spend some time feeling into all those Wild Dreams and whatever else you wrote down. i want you to choose or create five Wild Dreams that you would LOVE to accomplish—if it weren't for the fact that they feel impossible (right now). Choose your five dreams in any way that feels good—pull tarot cards, go with your hut (heart + gut), make more lists, choose only the ones that scare the **** out of you, choose them all! The goal is to pick the ones that charge you up in some way, whether it's fear, disbelief, or excitement—go with the ones that jolt you awake.

7 When you have your list, transfer it to your index card. This is what i call the Index Card of Wild Dreams. This one is yours.

8 Keep your index card somewhere you can see it, read it, and carry it with you every single day. Let your Index Card of Wild Dreams galvanize you to make daily choices that will align with its energy. Keep it close as you will be returning to this list in the following chapters.

Designing Your Wild Dream Life

Now that you have a clear(er) picture of your Wild Dreams, let's amplify your Wild Dreams energy by carrying and expanding it over the entirety of your life.

YOU are inherently worthy of having everything you desire in this life—and all the lives to come. YOU deserve—just by simply being the miraculous being you intrinsically are—to live your Wild Dream Life now. Let's magick and alchemize it all in now.

PRAXIS: LIVING INTO YOUR WILD DREAMS

Now that you're armed with your Wild Dreams, return to your Archetype Card. This is Card #2 that you pulled as your transformation archetype (see page 33). You will also need your journal and a pen.

1 Pull your Archetype Card from the deck and place it in front of you. Place your Index Card of Wild Dreams next to it. Keep your curiosity in the intersection between your Index Card and your Archetype Card.

2 What would your tarot archetype do every day to make the dreams on your list come true? What about weekly? Monthly? Annually? Make a list of everything that comes through in your journal.

3 Think about real people who have achieved the Wild Dreams (or a variation of them) on your list, who also embody the energy of your tarot archetype. Go back through the Rolodex of your life and see if you can come up with any examples. Type your Wild Dreams into an online search engine, along with some qualities from your Archetype card, to see who comes up.

4 Drawing inspiration from these two lists, consider what are the actions, behaviors, and mindset shifts you can begin to implement and integrate into your life now? Write them down in your journal. Feel free to make your list longer than three!

5 From this moment forward, commit to doing at least three things on your list. Once they feel like a part of you and/or a habit, choose two more.

6 The way we design our Wild Dream Life is by living it first. So, repeat this praxis, again and again.

SELF-ASSESSMENT

i invite you to mark the beginnings of your journey with a gentle, loving reminder to be honest with yourself. Answer the following questions with a number from 1 to 10 (with 1 being the lowest and 10 being the highest). There are no wrong answers here. We ALL start somewhere and this is where your transformation story begins.

How much do i believe in magick?

1 2 3 4 5 6 7 8 9 10

How much do i believe in MY personal medicine and magick?

1 2 3 4 5 6 7 8 9 10

How confident do i feel in my power to change my life?

1 2 3 4 5 6 7 8 9 10

How ready do i feel to begin moving my life in the direction of my Wild Dreams?

1 2 3 4 5 6 7 8 9 10

How confident do i feel in my ability, devotion, and consistency to achieve my Wild Dreams?

1 2 3 4 5 6 7 8 9 10

How much do i believe that magick can be a tool to help me achieve my Wild Dreams?

1 2 3 4 5 6 7 8 9 10

How ready am i, right now, to change my life?

1 2 3 4 5 6 7 8 9 10

Wild Dreams, Magick, and You

You are here for a reason. You chose this book because something inside you—consciously or not—was ready to transform your life in a holistic, intersectional, deeply poetic, and meaningful way. We have spent the previous pages laying a solid foundation and tilling the soil for the magick. Now, we are about to embark on to work in service to our highest good.

You have so much power in your toolbox already. Magick, transformation, and Wild Dreams are all here ready to be of service to you. To help guide and assist you as you make your way into the life, magick, and work you always dreamed and believed you would do. Thank you. Thank you. Thank you.

As we move through the rest of the book, i want you to keep your Guiding Card (Card #1, see page 19), your Archetype Card (Card #2, see page 33), and your Wild Dream Ally (Card #3, see page 39) front and center. Take a moment now to gather them into one place. Place your Index Card of Wild Dreams (see page 42) and your Proof List (see page 38) next to the cards.

Really take it all in—the journey you've already been on, the powerful discoveries you've made, the Wild Dreams you've dreamt, all the amazing hard things you've already done, and all the archetypes and support that has already come your way. Bow your head and heart in gratitude for everything that has shown up for you.

Take some time to sit with them—these are your Wild Dreams, your supportive guides and allies, your amazing life all right there in front of you. Stare in awe and amazement at the life you've already created for yourself. Stay in wild curiosity about them all— individually, collectively, universally.

PRAXIS: You have all your tools before you. Now, grab your pen and journal to capture everything they are trying to say.

1 Spend about 10 minutes listing out all the things you are grateful for—in your life, in the learning, lessons, and medicine of this book, any and all of it.

2 When you're done with your gratitude list, turn to a new page and return to all the magick you have in front of you—your cards, your Proof List, and your Index Card. What do they all have in common? What kinds of relationships and conversations are the cards having with each other?

3 Keep mixing and matching until you reach a point where your and their energy feels and says, *no mas*. There's nothing more. Trust that you have done and captured everything you needed.

4 You are now ready. It's time to go all in. Sign your name below in commitment to yourself, your magick, your transformation and to the creation and duration of your Wild Dreams.

_____

And so it is.
Let's begin.

PART I:

Preparing for Your Journey

And so you begin. On the following pages, you'll learn the fundamental skills of magick as you prepare for your quest for personal transformation. To help ground our learning, we call in from the Aztec Medicine Wheel (see page 98) the element of Earth, the medicine of Cihuatlāmpa (West), and their animal ally of wisdom, Snake. They will help to steady you as you build your knowledge base, test your skillsets, and praxis your way toward mastery—all the while, knowing that complete mastery is an illusion.

And so it is. Thank you. Thank you. Thank you.

Magickal Skills for Transformation

As above so below. As below as above. As within so without.
With you betwixt and between, landing from your leap,
there in front of you on the table is all you'll ever need.
With wisdom wrapped around you and infinity on your side,
you begin the quest of honing your magickal skillsets
and becoming The Magician of your life.

I THE MAGICIAN

Your Magickal Skillset

In the previous chapter, we got clear on what magick, transformation, and Wild Dreams are, while also rediscovering our own. You've gained some allies: tarot cards, lists, and a Wild-Dream-infused index card. Keep those nearby as you continue—everything will begin to alchemize from here.

On the following pages, i share with you nine skills, which work together in tandem to create the foundation of any magickal practice. i recommend you build a reliable relationship with each skill before attempting ritual or spellwork. Any one of these nine skills—when approached with care, intention, and focus—are magick, in and of themselves. i believe our magick, from the moment we begin our conscious practice of it, has the power to transform us from the inside out. Trust yourself and your relationship to magick to know when you're ready to move on in your journey. But remember to take your time.

If you have not already done so, i suggest you keep your journal handy, devoted to recording any sensations, reflections, and epiphanies you have as you read and work through each of the skills. This journal will become your grimoire (see page 89). Alright, friends. Let's begin.

Energy

Energy is an invisible driving force that animates and enlivens all things. Everything is energy. Energy IS life.

Energy as a magickal skill refers to our ability to be in an agency-sourced relationship to the energy we are trying to manipulate with our magick. As we know from the principle of vibration and law of conservation (see the Seven Hermetic Principles, page 80), energy "can neither be created nor destroyed—only converted from one form of energy to another." At its base level, magick is about influencing and directing energy (converting energy from one thing to another) via our will. But it's also much more metaphysical than that. Energy combines, twines, and weaves all elements together to create something wholly and holistically new.

Energy is the alpha of magick and the bedrock of the other eight foundational tools. From your ability to cast a spell with intention to what you call in and ward out when you cast a circle, energy is the baseline of it all. Energy is the basis of ALL magick. And your attention to, relationship with, and understanding of energy will impact the potency, quality, and longevity of it.

Most of us know and relate to energy as something that we have or don't have enough of. As we dive into energy as a skill, and as we move through the remainder of the book, i invite you to pay close attention to your own energy in your journal, from the impact you make when you enter a room to the imprint you leave behind.

While there are limitless forms that energy can take, on the following pages i want to call our attention to the three main energy forms we will be working and sharpening our skills with during your magickal transformation: Personal Energy, Universal Energy, and Elemental Energy.

Personal Energy

Your personal energy is the one that you carry with you unconsciously. The quality you take on when you are doing magickal (and really, any kind) of work. Personal energy is the frequency you emit, also known as your vibe, or personal energy signature. Each of us has our own unique energy signature made up of the things we believe, value, and think, the actions we take, and what we're passionate about—all the essential things that make us, us. Your personal energy signature dictates everything else—your emotions and your perspective on the world.

Universal Energy

This kind of energy is typically known as Higher Power, Spirit, Source, Divine, or God. Universal Energy can be found in places where natural energy collects, like in our bodies or within the Earth itself. These "power spots" can be found in universal environments, such as the intersection of ley lines (invisible lines that connect ancient mythical structures and landmarks), or in places such as Stonehenge, the Egyptian Pyramids, and the Pyramid of Sun and Moon in Teotihuacán, Mexico.

Power spots can also be found in your personal environment. Perhaps a city, or a place in your city, calls to you for no apparent reason (Truth or Consequences in New Mexico—and New Mexico in general—is one for me). Or perhaps there is a particular space in your home, or even objects in your home, that hold a certain energy only you can feel and fully understand. The natural wood writing desk i've had since my 20s is one of my personal power spots.

Elemental Energy

This is the energy of the natural world around us, such as the four elements of Fire, Water, Earth, and Air (or six, including Wood and Metal, depending upon your lineage). Elemental energy can be felt in the tools you work with, like your tarot and oracle decks and pendulums.

Strengthen Your Energy Skills

It's important to familiarize yourself with the types of energy you'll be working with as tools for your transformation and to identify the variations that will support you the most during your metamorphosis. In any magickal work, there are several variations of energy at play. All these energies work together to make or break your spell.

The energy you bring to the work: This is your personal energy signature mixed with your current emotional state. i recommend you come to your magickal work in a neutral state rather than emotionally charged. The more control you have over yourself, the more control you will have over your spells.

The energy of your intention: This is so important, i've made it a separate skill! You'll learn about intention next (see page 56).

The energy of the tool you are working with: We touched upon this in describing universal energy (see opposite). All your magickal tools—altars, altar cloths, candles, journals— have their own distinct energy profile.

The energy you're trying to call in: The thing you are trying to manifest holds its own unique energy. More often than not, we must adjust our frequency to match the energy of that which we are magicking to receive.

This praxis on the following pages focuses on developing your skills in the arena of your personal energy. The strength of this skill will influence all the others, including universal and elemental energies that we will cultivate specifically in the Tools section (see page 86).

PRAXIS: PERSONAL ENERGY MAP

This praxis will help you begin to understand your energy patterns and rhythms so you can work with them, not against them. You may wish to start on the New Moon and track an entire moon phase. Another variation is to begin on a Solstice or Equinox and track your energy for an entire seasonal cycle.

1 Grab your journal, open to a new page, and write the numbers 1–31 on the left-hand side. If, like me, you need more room to reflect and write, feel free to leave space between the lines. Today serves as Day 1.

2 Now open your favorite Moon phases app—my favs are Chani and Time Passages (see Resources, page 141). Write down the phase and sign Moon is in next to Day 1.

3 As you go about your day, pay attention to how you're feeling.

4 At the end of the day, write a word or a few sentences to describe how you felt. Describe the quality and level of your own energy, and the day's overall vibe and frequency. Write down your energy levels without judgment. When you feel complete, you are done.

5 Repeat steps 1–4 for the next 30 days.

6 At the end of the 30 days, take some time to reflect on the big picture of your energy. Ask yourself questions. Get curious. Play with this praxis and come up with unique ways to track your energy rhythms. If you start to see a pattern developing, you might choose to test it out in the next Moon cycle.

PRAXIS: BODY ENERGY CENTERS

There are multiple ways to see and develop a relationship with your body's energy system. Many of us have heard of the Hindu chakra system, but what about Chinese medicine's Meridians? Or Qigongs Dantians? Or the ancient Egyptian concept of Ka? What about your culture? Do your ancestors have a belief about your body's energy system?

1 Do some research on various body energy systems and begin to develop a relationship with your own energy centers. Begin the conversation with your body with a class—perhaps a Yin yoga class, which works deeply with your body's meridian system, or a Qigong class to feel into your lower and middle Dantians. Alternatively, try a meditation that focuses on the chakra system—find one that takes you through all seven chakras in your body so you can feel into each one.

2 As you move through these body practices (and hopefully others you find), journal your thoughts and discoveries about the movements and sensations you experience. Which energy centers feel most true to you in your own body? Continue to explore and build a relationship with those energy centers.

3 Once you begin to play, manipulate, and work with your body's energy system, you will organically begin to shift your personal energetic signature toward one with a higher voltage and frequency. This means you are becoming more congruent with your highest self and magick will naturally unfold from this place.

4 Jot down in your journal the changes you are noticing. What has caused the shifts to happen? Keep experimenting until you find the centers that feel most true for you.

Intention

Consciously or not, we create our lives through the choices we make. We can build a life of choices made in "response to" the people, systems, and environment around us or we can build a life of choices made in asking ourselves questions. What is it that i truly want? What is it that i truly intend for myself, my work, my life? Our honest answers to these questions help us create the life we desire. Focusing our Intention is what will help us get there. Intention is the target you are aiming for, the end game you're envisioning, and the plan you desire (or intend) to act out.

There's a saying that goes, "Where your attention goes, energy flows." While this is true, i would add that intention is a necessary prerequisite for both. Intention directs attention. Attention then points energy in the right direction to flow. In this way, the roots of our life are seeded in our intentions.

Intention is the energy that animates our actions and, when we work with intention(s), we are working with the base level energy of anything we are divinely trying to conjure up. Having, knowing, and rooting our intention can make or break any manifestation or goal, let alone our spellwork. That's because your intentions are your inspiration. Like your Wild Dreams, your intentions become your driving "Why?" because they are deeply personal and radically connected to your soul. Intention opens the gate for magick to flow in and through.

As a magickal skill, intention is one of your most powerful wands. With magickal skill, you consciously set, aim, and then fire your intention out into the Universe by imbuing it with your power, focus, and love. Intention is the vehicle through which you weld your will and manifest your magick.

The praxises that follow were designed to help you reclaim the power of intention by directing its energy back onto you.

PRAXIS: SNOWBALL OF INTENTION

Grab your journal and a pen for this praxis. As you move through each step, allow each prompt to organically move you to the next. Allow yourself to ride the energy waves of momentum. Allow each answer to snowball into the next question. Then the next. Then the next.

1 Begin with grounding. Take three deep breaths. Allow each one to cleanse and open up space in you to receive.

2 Consider your intention right now, at this moment. Let the sensation linger in your mind and body, listening for what comes up. When you feel something—a word, emotion, sentence, energy—write it down.

3 What is your intention for this praxis? Repeat the receptive praxis in step 2.

4 What is your intention for this book? Repeat step 2.

5 What is your intention for your day? Repeat step 2.

6 What is your intention for your week? Repeat step 2.

7 What is your intention for your month? Repeat step 2.

8 What is your intention for your life? Repeat step 2.

9 Whatever you received, whatever you wrote down, let that be enough. Because it is. The praxis is complete.

PRAXIS: RITUAL OF DAILY INTENDING

The moments immediately after you wake up are the most potent moments of the day. This praxis works with that time to create a simple but profound waking spell. By doing this ritual first thing in the morning, you are beginning your day with the frequency and energy that you desire to call in. Start tomorrow to infuse your day with more of what you want!

1 The moment you open your eyes, before you do anything else—make your coffee, get the kids or partner ready for the day, brush your teeth, pick up your phone, ANYTHING—give thanks for the new day and set an intention. Doing it before you step out of bed aligns and infuses your first steps into your new day with your unique intention.

2 Your intention for the day can be anything you want. Some mornings my intention is a word like "abundant." Sometimes it's a vibe like "presence."

Sometimes it's a feeling like "feeling good." My morning ritual of intending has also included tarot cards, people whose vibe i admire and want to be more like, astrology signs, Aztec deities, Disney characters, authors, and so much more.

3 Once you have something, speak it out loud. (If you're concerned about waking your partner up, whisper it before you leave the bed and then, once outside and beyond hearing range, say it out loud.) By stating your Intention out loud you are attuning your vibe to it in a very tangible way—and that's a powerful way to start your day.

Belief

What is belief? Faith and trust. A solid, unshakable sense of knowing. You don't have to see something first to know (or believe) it's true.

We must believe to achieve. Because believing creates the seeing—and then the doing, thinking, and receiving. When we plug into our belief—in ourselves, in our power, in our abilities—we unleash an avalanche of opportunities in our lives. We make more room for creativity, magick, and miracles.

Belief is a collection of energy made up of the stories, thoughts, and words you say to yourself regularly. You can tell yourself things that reinforce self-belief or things that deflate it. That's because belief is neutral—it will attach itself to wherever you energetically intend it to go (which is why the first two skills of energy and intention are so important!).

Your beliefs—specifically the ones that come from the stories and words you tell yourself—can be changed. Your beliefs will go wherever you steer them. That itself is magick!

The Magick of Belief

Belief in yourself is the ultimate superpower. Your magick is built on the shoulders of your belief. First, you must believe in magick in order to use it. Next, you must believe in your power and ability to be a conduit for magick. Then (and most importantly), you must believe in your own manifesting power to conjure your manifestations true. Belief is the force behind it all. Belief transforms you into the most powerful magick maker in the world. Your belief in your own abilities affect the frequency and result of everything you want in life. Belief contains the power of the Universe and within that Universal power comes our ability to be the Sacred Creatrixes (sacred and sovereign creators) of our lives.

Follow the praxis on the following pages to help you build an unshakable belief in yourself and your magick.

PRAXIS: "I BELIEVE" MANTRAS

Believing in ourselves isn't always the easiest thing to do. Belief is a powerful spell you must consciously spin for yourself. Luckily for us, belief can be built. The more we practice it the stronger it becomes. Grab a pen and paper (or your journal) to create powerful mantras that will support you as you build self-belief.

1 Pull out your "My Proof List" (see page 38) and identity something on the list you have already done. If you haven't completed that praxis yet, go back and create your list before moving on.

2 Write down on the sheet of paper what you had to believe for that thing to manifest. Because you had to believe something about yourself and your skills or talents for the things on your list to come true.

3 Now turn each of your "i had to believe" into an "i believe" mantra. Your goal is to create short, inspiring phrases that leave you feeling empowered. How you get there is up to you. You cannot get this wrong.

4 When you're done, celebrate! You just created an "i Believe List" full of mantras you can use to support you and your self-belief as you continue to reach for and catch your Wild Dreams!

PRAXIS: WHAT DO I BELIEVE?

Grab your journal for this powerful praxis, which will help you to ensure your beliefs are supporting your quest for magick. Return to it again and again and adjust as often as needed to help make all your Wild Dreams come true.

1 Set a timer for 30 minutes and in your journal riff your answers to the following questions:

- What beliefs do i hold about the world?

- What beliefs do i hold about myself?

- What beliefs do i hold about magick?

- What beliefs do i hold about what is (and is not) possible for me?

2 Look at what you have written and for each of your answers, ask yourself: "Why do i believe this? Was it a belief that someone taught me? Was it learned? Something i discovered or experienced myself?" The goal of these questions is to see if you can get to the core and roots of your beliefs.

3 For each belief on your list, ask yourself another question: "Is this belief helping or hindering me?" Get honest. Keep it real. Stay in self-love. If you find your belief is helping you, how can you reinforce it?

4 If you find your belief is hindering you, ask yourself, "Is this something i still want to believe?" If the answer is yes, then honor that—you are still exactly where you need to be (but make a note to check back in with this belief after you finish this book to see if anything has changed).

5 If your answer is no, consider what can be shifted. Is it the system? Is it the situation or circumstance? Is it me? Is it my perspective and perception? (Hint: it almost always is.) Ask yourself, "What empowering belief can i replace it with?"

Mindset

Mindset is the gateway to success. Your mindset is the culmination of the three skills—energy, intention, and belief—that came before it. The intensity and vibration of these skills open the way for the four skills—manifesting, spiritual will, congruency, and self-rule—that follow.

Mindset is both a doorway to your next level life and a reflection of why you are living your current one. That's because your mindset is made up of all your thoughts—the stories you tell yourself, the way you talk to yourself, and the beliefs you hold about the world and your role in it. Mindset is also the result of what you feed it, from the media, news, and stories you consume to the people you surround yourself with.

Your mindset is the lens through which you view everything. It is the culmination of all your thoughts and stories and what you make them mean. It is reason why you behave, act, and react the way you do, and it is behind the choices you make (or don't make). Your mindset can make your life or break it. Which way your life pendulum swings is a choice. Mindset is always up to you.

Change Your Mind,
Transform Your Life

You/i/we/us have no control over anybody else, or what they do with their bodies, access, or power. We can, however, control what we make it mean in our life. i cannot directly control the inequities and inequality that happen on a systemic level, but i can take back my power and rewrite what injustice means in my life. i adopt a mindset of "the personal is political" and spiritual activism and follow it up with action.

Your mindset is the personal magick you do on you. It's the spell you cast on yourself every time you form a belief about something, use certain words to describe yourself or your life (whether vocally or just in your head), or what you decide to make something mean, whether your interpretation is positive, negative, or neutral. Your mindset is the most powerful tool in your arsenal, the magickal, mystical force working behind the scenes of everything you do—or don't do. It is the key that unlocks your agency, power, and magick—and continues to nourish it.

When you reclaim the power of mindset on a personal level, its effects directly and proportionately ripple out. Your mindset affects your partner, your family, and your friends, which in turn affects the people they know. The seeds that begins in your mind and blooms via your mindset can pollinate the world. And that is real magick.

But to change anything, we must first adopt the mindset that it can be done . . . and that you/i/we/us are the ones to do it.

PRAXIS: MINDSET SELF-MAGICK

There's a variety of praxis that will help you to take back control of your mind. Below are a few that i love and use almost every day—choose one to implement for the next 30-40 days. Reflect on any shifts that occurred and then layer a new one on top. Continue until you find a recipe that creates the kind of mindset you want and need.

Meditation: This doesn't have to mean sitting in stillness. Meditation can look like walking, dancing, or anything that draws your attention inward.

Gratitude: i make lists of 5-10 things i'm grateful for every day. Real, deep, thoughtful gratefulness for the bounty in your life keeps mindset in the frequency of abundance—something i am always working on cultivating.

Smiling: Just one minute of smiling every morning is an instant energy and mindset shifter!

Mantras and affirmations: i often remind myself—both aloud and in my head—who i want to become. Affirmations help me direct my mind's energy to the success i'm seeking. Mantras reaffirm that which i desire to call in or are a reminder of what i already have.

Tapping: More about this in our next praxis (see opposite).

PRAXIS: EFT (TAPPING)

One of my favorite tools to quickly and profoundly up-level my mindset is Tapping, known as EFT (Emotional Freedom Technique), which consists of literally tapping with your fingers on different points of your body. For this praxis, i want you to try out tapping for at least a week. i've also created several special tapping videos for you to tap along with me (see Resources, page 141).

1 Tapping usually begins with what's called a "set-up," where we speak out loud about our issues and problems while tapping on the fleshy part on the side of our hand.

2 During the set-up, we also reinforce our love for ourselves, despite all our negative feelings. This is often stated as, "Even though X, Y, Z [enter negative thoughts and feelings here], i deeply and completely love, accept, and forgive myself." The set-up helps us get into a state where we acknowledge what is going on so that we can then move through it.

3 Tapping on each of these points is considered one round of tapping. While there are a few variations of the tapping points, these are the nine i follow:

- Top of the head (your crown area)
- Start of the eyebrows (just above the brow line)
- Temples (on each side of your head)
- Under the eyes (toward the middle of each)
- Under the nose (in the space between your nose and lips)
- Under the mouth (in that crevice of your chin)
- Collarbones (slightly below the bones)
- Under the armpit (slightly below the space where a bra might sit)
- Wrists together

Manifesting

Manifesting and magick are two sides of the same coin. Manifesting invites magick in. Whenever we are working with spells, incantations, New Moon Intention setting, or any aspect of our magick, we are working in the realm of manifesting.

At its most basic level, manifesting means to make something real. Everything that surrounds you/i/we/us was once an impossibility in someone's mind until they believed in themselves and their manifestation power so strongly that they made it so. Manifestation is an impossibility made possible. Manifestation is a gift from Great Spirit to us all. It is a cornerstone of humxnity because we were born to create—art, businesses, spaghetti, music, dances, love, chai tea lattes, iPhones, technology, tiny humxns—and innovate all aspects of life. We were born to make something out of nothing. To take energy, as it exists in one form, and transform it into another. We are proof of big magick, tall tales made flesh, and Wild Dreams come true. Manifesting is a skill we are all innately born with. However, most of us have forgotten how to use it.

Having a clear understanding of how you best manifest is a key component to unlocking the power behind your magick work. The praxises that follow are intended to help you (re) discover your particular way of manifesting by working with two systems: the Three Steps and the Nine Pillars of Manifestation (see page 68).

The Three Steps

Pop culture and popular books on manifestation have taught us that the three main steps to manifesting are 1. Ask, 2. Believe, 3. Receive. In the following praxis, we are trying on these three traditional steps. The goal isn't to "test" ourselves or the Universe but to consciously build and strengthen our manifesting muscle. Start small and keep your manifestation asks simple and easy for now.

PRAXIS: 40 DAYS OF MANIFESTATION

Why 40 days? In spirituality, 40 is a mystical number. In Buddhism, Siddhartha Gautama (later known as Buddha) meditated for 40 days under a Bodhi Tree without food or water to achieve enlightenment. The planet Venus retrogrades for 40 days and 40 nights every 18 months. Jesus spent 40 days and 40 nights in the desert alone. Forty is a number of transformation—which is exactly what we're trying to do.

1 Take a moment to rate your belief in your manifesting ability on a scale of 1 to 10, with 1 being the lowest and 10 the highest.

2 The following morning, before you start your day, tell the Universe what you would like to manifest (see below for suggestions). Keep it achievable and make it something that can be manifested in a day. Your choices are endless! Get creative.

3 Ask the Universe to help you ... and stay open to your manifestations showing up in surprising and unexpected ways!

4 Each day, for the next 40 days, choose one new thing to manifest into your life.

5 Once you've completed your first 40 days, rate yourself again. See how the numbers have shifted—i promise you they will!

YOU COULD MANIFEST ...

- A random penny or other coin
- A free cup of coffee
- A phone call from a friend (or someone else you haven't heard from in a while)
- A particular bird or animal—like a butterfly, owl, or wolf
- A particular song to pop up on your random playlist
- A new book, notebook, or journal
- A free ticket to an event you want to attend
- A certain tarot card to pop up in your day

The Woke Magick Nine Pillars of Manifesting

While i believe the three steps are a wonderful place to start, i don't believe it is the most powerful (or empowering) method of manifesting. As a witch who exists in the locus of many intersections—bisected by and living in systemic oppression and inequality—i have found the most impactful method is inclusive of both surrender and personal agency while also leaving room for magick and the miraculous to come in.

Over my decades of manifesting everything, from becoming a drag queen and securing book deals to meeting the love of my life and developing my relationship with Spirit and money, i've discovered a unique, agency-inclusive approach to manifesting that i want to introduce you to. It's called the Woke Magick Nine Pillars of Manifesting, which can be explored in the following praxis.

PRAXIS: EMBODY THE NINE PILLARS

For this praxis, choose one thing you want to manifest and work through each of the Woke Magick Nine Pillars of Manifesting to achieve it. In this praxis, i offer the example of an extra $1,000 in one week. Make sure that whatever steps (or pillars) you choose, they align with your values (we'll dive deeper into this in Congruency, see page 78) and that it feels good—energetically, spiritually, and morally—to you.

1 Know: You must know yourself, what your Wild Dreams are, and why you want to transform into someone who can manifest them. Clearly state what you want to manifest. For example, "i will manifest an extra $1,000 this week."

2 Believe: You've GOT to believe in manifestation. Deepen your belief that manifestation is possible by revisiting the belief affirmations you created (see page 61), doing a round of tapping (see page 65), and returning to your "My Proof List" (see page 38) as a reminder of all the badass sh*t you've done. The goal here is to root your belief in your bones.

3 Clarify and focus: Get crystal clear about your desires and the focus needed to manifest them. Don't muddle your desire with unstable energy—stay in the truth that an extra $1,000 is possible for you. From this place of clear presence, we ask the Universe: "i want to manifest an extra $1,000 this week. Will you help me?"

4 Prepare and align: Gather the support and resources you need to achieve your $1,000 goal. Pull a supportive tarot card for the journey. Prepare your mindset. Give gratitude to the money you currently have in your bank account. Feel into whatever else your manifestation wants or needs. Point and align all of them to your chosen dream.

5 Map: Plan your strategy and set milestones along the route. Ask yourself "How can i do my part?" Maybe you could pick up an extra shift or follow up on an overdue invoice. Brain- and heart-storm ways that you can meet the Universe halfway.

6 Spirit: How will reaching your $1,000 goal happen? Invite Spirit, your guides, and ancestors to help, assist, or venture on this journey with you. Ask them to carry the burden of "how" for you so you can remain free and open to the muse and Spirit.

7 Inspirited action: Take inspirited action and track it. Follow your Light Rabbits (see below). Do a few things you wrote down in the heart-storm list you created in Step 5. Keep a tab in your journal of the amount of money you receive in gift or cash form at the end of the day. Give gratitude and thanks to all that has come in.

8 Allow and receive: Be open to the miraculous, allow grace to happen, and receive every single bounty you encounter along the way. Your $1,000 can come from anywhere—a random check in the mail, a refund to your bank account, a stranger at a bar—because it can and does happen. In fact, all these are examples of money miracles happening in my life.

9 Review and adjust: At the end of the week, add it all up. Did you manifest your $1,000? Less? More? Take some time to reflect on your manifesting journey. This is how we learn about our nuances in manifesting. Course-correct and adjust your sails as often as needed. Some questions you could ask yourself are:

- How and where did my money show up?

- What Light Rabbits did i follow that had the most impact?

- What money miracles did i experience?

- Did my belief ebb and flow throughout the week? If so, what triggered it?

- How was my mindset? What helped me stay in an aligned? What distracted me?

LIGHT RABBITS

Light Rabbits are what i call those pings, hunches, or "aha!" moments. They are those ideas that have a particular shine, shimmer, or glimmer to them. They are an inkling that we have to take a particular action right now or go a certain way. Follow any Light Rabbits you receive while in manifestation mode.

Sensing

You enter a room and all the hairs on your body stand up. You jog through the park, and something implores you to run the other way. You're walking from your bedroom to the bathroom, feel a cold gush of wind at your back, and quickly turn the lights on.

These are all real instances where you are organically and intuitively sensing the energy around you and then acting accordingly. We tap into our bodily and sensory sensations and know something is true without needing outside validation or proof. You've unconsciously bypassed your brain and dropped into the realm of feeling and sensing— where all magick lives.

Sensing is being fully present in your body. So much so, that you can pick up on the vibration of all the elements around you—your teacup, your desk, the fabric on your skin, even the shivers of energy bubbling up, activating, and flowing through your body. Sensing is paying radical attention to the nepantla (the liminal space that exists between all things) and what happens while we are in that space.

i feel. Therefore i know. As a magickal skill, sensing is your ability to feel into and know what is right for a particular spell, a certain tarot spread, or an herbal ingredient for healing without a spell or recipe book. This combination of feeling and knowing is the foundation of our intuition—it is its first, active component. You sense, you intuit, and then you act. Your ability to sense subtle energy shifts, intentionally and on command, is the adeptness i want to help you cultivate on the following pages.

One of my favorite ways to practice intuitive sensing is with an app called Extra Sense (see Resources, page 141). You can download it free on your Apple or Android phone. Just choose a game and begin—you'll be instantly hooked!

Clair Senses

Sensing is your body's direct line of communication with Spirit. How we take in information and impressions from energy and the spirit world is known as the clair senses— intuitive and psychic abilities that often correlate to our five senses. Although they are not directly related to physical ability, the clairs are ways that we receive and interpret shifts in energy, whatever space we are in.

Clairvoyance (or clear seeing), such as flashes, images, and pictures in your mind's eye or your chosen scrying object, is one of the more well-known clairs. Again, clairvoyance and "seeing" are not linked with the physical ability and sense of sight. Folxs "see" in a myriad of ways. You do not need to be sight able-bodied to tap into this clair. Other examples include clairaudience (clear hearing), clairgustance (clear tasting), and clairsalience (clear smelling). Claircognizance (clear knowing) is a sense of very solid and unshakable information that pops into your head without really knowing why or where it came from, and with no prior knowledge or access. Clairsentience (clear feeling) is the ability to feel and sense other people's energies, like their fears, insecurities, or jealousy. Clearsentients can also feel the emotional pain of the land or space where wars, murders, colonization, and other atrocities have happened.

These are just some of the many clairs that we have access to. And while we all have some clairs that come more naturally than others, the following praxis will help you to experience and strengthen them all.

PRAXIS: STRENGTHENING YOUR CLAIR SENSES

Inspired by Dani Shapiro's daily writing exercise (see Resources, page 141), all you need for this praxis is a pen and your journal. The goal of this praxis is to build a relationship with, become more aware of, and use your clairs on a day-to-day basis. If you find that you have a clair or two that is more naturally developed, switch out their respective quadrants for a clair you would like to cultivate.

1 In your journal, divide a page into four quadrants or squares by drawing a line vertically and then horizontally across the page.

2 On the top left upper quadrant, write the word "See." Inside this quadrant, leave space to make a list of seven things you will sense visually throughout the day.

3 On the top right upper quadrant, write the word "Hear." In this quadrant, you will make a list of seven things you sense audibly throughout the day.

4 On the bottom left quadrant, write the word "Know." Here, you will write down one thing you knew for sure during the day.

5 Throughout the day, remain aware of these three clairs, and complete each quadrant as you experience each one. If you can't come up with seven things for a particular clair, list what you have and make a note to focus on that specific clair tomorrow.

6 In the evening, write the word "channel" in the bottom right quadrant. Set a timer for 5–10 minutes and either channel write, doodle, or draw something you sensed throughout the day.

PRAXIS: SENSING THE DAY'S ENERGY

Set aside at least five minutes at the beginning of the day to activate and enliven your intuition. This praxis is most effective when practiced over a consecutive duration of time (i recommend at least 40 days). The more you do this praxis, the more attuned your sensing antennas will become—and the more powerful your intuition will be.

1 Close your eyes and drop your consciousness into your body.

2 Begin to sense by feeling the energy around you. To help put into words what you are sensing, here are a few questions you can ask yourself:

- What does it feel like?

- What flavor is it?

- Is there a particular color or texture that is associated with the day?

- What can you see?

- Do you hear or smell anything?

3 Are there any energies (that aren't yet present) that you would like to call in? Maybe it's the energy of the intention you set when you first woke up. Maybe it's the energy you need to motivate you to make that hard phone call or ask. Whatever energy you need to invoke to assist you in what you have planned, invite it to weave itself into your day during this praxis.

4 Open your eyes, jot down any notes or things you want to remember in your journal, and go about your day.

5 Before you go to sleep at night, look at what you felt and called in. Match your notes to what showed up for you throughout the day. How was it different? How was it the same? Did any clairs show up instinctively or consistently?

Spiritual Will

Spiritual will is power. If you're ever wondering where the potency of your spell comes from, look no further than the degree, intensity, and consistency of your spiritual will.

Spiritual will is the most formidable force alive in you. It's your soul drive—that underlying, undeniable, and untouchable force made from the magickal mix of determination, spirit, desire, and focus that naturally resides in you. It is the driving force behind your magick and the frequency dictating how quickly your manifestations, wishes, and Wild Dreams come to you. Your will is your word. Your word is your wand. Your wand is your will made flesh. This is most powerful incantation in magick:

"And so it is."

Why? Because you are invoking into your existence your will and desires without question or hesitancy of it coming true. By invoking unbreakable belief with your spiritual will, you've invited Spirit in to help open and pave the way. You have spoken, and in doing so, turned the spell over to Great Spirit. You willed it. Gave it over to the Universe. And so it is.

Your spiritual will is how you meet Spirit halfway. It is how the metaphysical—the thoughts, energies, and actions you choose—interact, manipulate, and manifest in the physical world through you. Your spiritual will is the main ingredient you bring to every spell, the magick, the energy, and the frequency that sets your spell in motion. Spiritual will is your magickal power. And in the following praxis, you are going to work on making your spiritual will the most dynamic it can be.

PRAXIS: FOLLOW THROUGH

Doing this praxis regularly helps me reclaim all the power i'm leaking out by not following through on my words with action. i do this praxis—which takes place over one whole week— every season. For this week, there is NO tomorrow. Only today. This praxis isn't as easy as it sounds, but of all the praxis in this book, this one alone will change your life. It will shift your magick if you commit to it fully. So go do it!

1 Do what you say you're going to do. If you run across an old friend and catch yourself saying, "i'll call you soon," then reach out to them the next day. If you say you're going to start eating more vegan meals, cut out all animal products in your next meal. If you write something in your calendar or on your to-do list, do whatever it takes to get it done. Be relentless. Do not go to sleep. Do not pass go. Do not collect $200 until you have done and finished everything you set out to do. Period.

2 If you really don't want to do something, don't say you're going to do it. How many times while reading this book did you say to yourself, i'm going to do this praxis only to fall into the trap of "later" or tomorrow? Probably more than you care to admit. It's so easy to slip back into the old pattern of saying casualties just to be nice or in passing without any real intention of doing them. You'll quickly learn how much energy you've unconsciously been leaking from your spiritual will. Your magick knows, feels, and responds to that lack of spiritual will accordingly. We cannot expect our magick to be powerful enough to get the results we want if we cannot trust ourselves to have the decisive will to do the small things.

PRAXIS: WILL IT INTO EXISTENCE

Often, we believe that something is never going to happen or abdicate our power to others in hopes that they will make it happen. The goal of this praxis is to get into the habit of willing something into existence. While this is advanced manifesting magick, i believe in your ability to do what you will yourself to do. It requires practice—it may not happen as quickly as we want or expect it to. Or maybe it will.

This praxis is based on my own experience of willing experiences into my life (see page 35). But it's not just me. Many others, from MVP Quarterbacks to neurodivergent witches to single mothers, have conjured the power of their will to manifest their desires, goals, and Wild Dreams into being.

1 Pick one Wild Dream you have from your Index Card of Wild Dreams (see page 42).

2 i want you to will it into existence. How do we do this? Not just by acting as if it has already happened, but by living as if it's already happening. This strengthens your spiritual will by putting physical world action behind it. It tells the Universe you are so serious about getting what you want that you're willing to do whatever it takes to achieve and experience it now.

3 Keep a journal of all the big and small things that have shown up in your life that relate to the Wild Dream you chose. Keep throwing everything you have at it until it comes true. Because it will.

Congruency

Congruency is our beliefs, morals, and values brought to life via our actions. i believe, therefore i act, henceforth (unto) i am. What you do is who you become—and who you become is the result of what you do.

Everything is connected; everything bleeds into each other. The way we tap into the power of all and everything is by riding the wave of congruency through it. By being a walking embodiment and model of what congruency looks like in our physical lives.

Congruency is both energetic—the true feelings and thoughts we think or say to ourselves—and physical—our actions, behaviors, and choices. When you are living a life of congruency, you are walking your talk, actioning your morals and values with every choice you make, and coming as close as you humxnly can to living your life in alignment with the laws that govern us all—in and out of magick.

When i became a vegetarian at age 16, i became congruent with my love of animals and my desire not to hurt them or add to their suffering. When i chose to lowercase my "i"s and fight for them to be published as is, i became congruent with my desire to decolonize myself. This kind of conscious aligned action, energy, and way of living shows up in my magick as degrees of potency and efficacy. The more i live in alignment with the Hermetic Principles (see page 80), my beliefs, and personal truths the stronger my magick is. And the more energized i become.

When we are congruent, we experience unbelievable synchronicities, daily unexplainable alignments, and radical authenticity that ignite the way to all our successes.

Congruency strengthens magick because it plugs up any energy leaks and fissures in our energy and therefore our magick. Congruency is the energetic skeletal system of our magick, amplifying and strengthening everything it touches, making you more of what you already are, and influencing your spiritual will and ability to manifest powerful magick. Congruency creates an impenetrable channel of energy that connects Great Spirit to the Universe to and through our body, ultimately spilling into our magickal tools, and out into our magick and manifestations. The more congruent we become, the more formidable our magick is.

A WORD OF CAUTION

No one is 100 per cent congruent in every aspect of their life. We are all humxn, we are all walking contradictions, and that's okay. Like the Universe, we—and our ability to be in radical alignment with all life—is ever-evolving and shifting. Our magick does not demand congruence perfection, only that we stay aware and do better than we did before. If we do our best, the Universe and our magick will respond accordingly.

THE SEVEN HERMETIC PRINCIPLES

Sometimes called, the Seven Natural Laws of the Universe (or Universal Laws for short), these seven principles—along with the Aztec Medicine Wheel and other Western Occult Esoteric texts—root my magick and guide my life (see page 13). The study of the Seven Hermetic Principles can last a lifetime. While the principles are a magickal praxis in and of themselves, you'll find an introduction and brief description of each principle below.

1 The Principle of Mentalism: Mind, the Universe, everything is mental—everything is energy. This is the principle that "your thoughts create your reality," the modern nomenclature that manifestation culture was born from.

2 The Principle of Correspondence: Any one thing contains everything else. All hierarchies are interconnected and relational. Separation is an illusion. i work with this principle throughout all my magickal workings (both in and out of this book) by holding it as a core philosophy and tenant of my magickal praxis.

3 The Principle of Vibration: Everything all around us is in a constant state of movement and holds a certain frequency and vibration—including us. The frequency and vibration (aka vibes) we emanate are under our control—we change our mind, we change our vibe. In Alchemy, this principle is known as transmutation, or changing from one state to another.

4 The Principle of Polarity: Opposites are two sides of the same coin. Again, separation is an illusion—everything is nothing and everything all at once. We are all walking contradictions with the ability to hold multiple truths at once.

5 The Principle of Rhythm: Everything has its own unique cadence made visible in various aspects of nature—the rising and setting of Sun, Moon phases, and seasonal changes. This is reflected in the ebb and flow of our lives, the inner workings of our bodies, and the natural rhythm of aging.

6 The Principle of Cause and Effect: This principle is found in mathematician and physicist (and astronomer, alchemist, and occultist) Isaac Newton's Third Law, which states, "for every action (force) in nature there is an equal and opposite reaction." We can also find it in the biblical adage of, "you reap what you sow."

7 The Principle of Gender: This law does not speak of socially constructed gender norms, those strict dichotomies of male/female or either/or that society demands we adhere to. Rather, the truth that everything and all (including us) contains all the energies of the other. This Principle of Gender circles back to the Principle of Polarity in that nothing—including gender—is an absolute. Everything that contains feminine energy also contains masculine and vice versa (which doesn't negate the fact that something can be more feminine or masculine energetically than the other). This is a subtle but VERY important energetic difference to understand as this principle does not promote socially constructed, heteronormative ideas of gender, but—in direct opposition—a more fluid and intersectional one.

PRAXIS: THE SEVEN HERMETIC PRINCIPLES

If we can stay in radical awareness and alignment with the Hermetic Principles when it comes to the tools and practice of our magick, then we will always find ourselves in congruency and right relationship with the Universe and what we are trying to call in.

1 Create a snapshot of what your life looks like now. Make note of how you're feeling, the numbers in your bank account, your mindset, and whatever else you want to track to see if and how it's changed or grown.

2 Review the Seven Hermetic Principles (see page 80). Choose one of the seven to focus on for the next week. The principle you choose will be the filter you run everything in your life through. Here are some inquiries to guide your exploration of the principle:

- How do i feel about this principle?

- Where and in what ways does this principle show up in my life?

- How am i living out this principle in my everyday life?

- In what ways am i congruent with this principle? In what ways am i not?

- Are my actions, thoughts, and behaviors in alignment with this principle? If not, how can i choose differently?

3 At the end of the week, reflect on what you've learned about the principle, yourself, and both in relationship to the other.

4 Is there any other exploration that wants to happen with this principle? If yes, follow what you are sensing. If not, pick another principle and begin again. Repeat this praxis until all seven principles have been accounted for.

5 When you've worked through them all, return to your snapshot and ask yourself, how have i changed? How has my life shifted? How am i more congruent with who i am—and who i want to be? Don't forget to celebrate!

PRAXIS: WEB OF CONGRUENCY

In this praxis, we are going to work on weaving channels of congruency in our lives. This is not about achieving 100 percent congruency. It's about becoming more aware of the energy of the things you bring into your life and the tools you bring into your magick. Keep your journal handy and make note of any triggers or emotions this praxis brings up for you.

1 Choose three of your favorite magickal tools. It could be your favorite crystal, tarot deck, candle, pendulum—whatever you like or use the most.

2 For each tool, write in your journal your answers to the following questions: What is the origin story of this tool? Where did it come from? How was it produced?

3 Close your eyes. See if you can feel and follow your chosen tool's energy to where, when, and how it began. What do you see, sense, and feel? Write that down too.

4 Who is the artist or maker of this tool? What was their energy and intention in creating it? Do you know if this tool is ethically sourced? If you don't know, that's totally okay. Take some time to do whatever research you need to complete your answers.

5 Review what you've written for all three tools and ask yourself: Is this in alignment with what i believe? Why or why not? If your tools are in alignment, great! Keep building upon your web of congruency. If they are not, that's wonderful information too—now you are more aware of where the lapse of congruency is, and you can make better choices next time.

Self-leadership

The secret of living a magickal life is living a self-led life. Magick is all about leading oneself back to your own power and ability (and responsibility) to be the creatrix of your own life.

You are a leader. The problem is, this truth has been buried under generations of conditioning. We live and learn within systems that teach us to turn over our power to "authorities." We have been silenced by the narrative that other people—not you!—know what's best for you. It's time to take your power and agency back.

Lead yourself back to the truth that you are a leader—right now, just as you are. Magick teaches us how to do that. Taking yourself through the transformations and praxises in this book is proof that you already know how to lead yourself. If you've made it this far in this book without taking any actions, i want you to choose one of the praxises you've already read, put the book down, and DO THE PRAXIS. This is self-leadership in action.

When you work with magick, there is no other source moving you into action but you. Spirit will always be there to meet you, but you must make the first move. The ability to make those first moves is what self-leadership looks like.

Self-leadership is a powerful force in your magick because it is the culmination of every skill in you—your spiritual will, your mindset, what you believe, your energy, the magnetism of your congruency—and how they manifest in your life via the choices you make and the actions you take. Your ability to direct and motivate yourself are all key components of self-leadership in magick.

And so it is, my friends.

And so shall you lead yourself to be.

PRAXIS: DECISIONS

The grand spell of our lives is made up of the individual choices we make. Decision-making IS magick-making. And therein lies all our power. Before you begin this praxis, take a moment to reflect on the last decision you made. How did you come to this decision? Was it a quick decision? Did you abdicate your power by letting someone else choose for you? Is the way you make decisions leaking your energy and power? Consider everything you can about the energy of your decision-making.

The manner and energy in which you make decisions in your life are a telltale sign of the health of your self-leadership skills. In this praxis, you are going to revolutionize your decision-making habit. The next time you must make a decision, i want you to:

1 Remember that you are a sacred, sovereign leader. Choose to begin making decisions in the fullness of your power.

2 Tap into your leadership power and make a definitive decision. Trust your instincts. No dancing around in what-ifs.

3 Take immediate action on the decision you made. Action solidifies your decision. And making conscious decisions is how we will lead ourselves to where we want to go.

PART II:

Your Magickal Tools for Transformation

In this metamorphic section, we call in from the Aztec Medicine Wheel (see page 98) the element of Water, the medicine of Huīzlāmpa (South), and their animal ally Hummingbird. They will help guide the flow of our intuition, creativity, and psychic ability as we become the winds of change in the ocean of our life.

And so it is. Thank you. Thank you. Thank you.

The Tools

Having honed your skills, conjured your creatrix,
and reclaimed your magick,
you stand before two pillars;
one of total transformation,
one of where you've always been.
The choice is yours,
your book of life in your hands, asking:
Will you stay as you arrived?
Stagnate as The Magician,
or transform into the High Priestess of your life?

i believe any tool—magickal or not—in which you choose to infuse your attention, intention, and energy holds a frequency and charge of transformation and change. On the following pages, i share nine magickal tools. They will help you to access the immensity of your magick and the enormity of your power, so you can breathe proof into what is possible for you.

Each tool opens with a story that was either directly channeled from Spirit (more about how to do this yourself later, see Spirit Writing page 119) or a channeled variation of the legends and myths of my ancestors. In my culture, storytelling is medicine. Stories take us out of our logical and thinking brains and drop us into our hearts—the place inside ourselves where we can access and do anything.

And i believe you can do, be, and/or have anything you want. It's time you believe it too. Let the magicking begin!

Grimoire

A grimoire is a sacred space and magickal ally that can help you to express, track, and reflect on your magick and transformation.

Traditionally, grimoires functioned as a personal record of magick. Hidden within any magician's grimoire pages could be ritual procedures and magickal correspondences, manifesting and conjuring instructions, recipes, and spells, as well as notes, passages, and downloads they receive from Spirit. All with the intent to pass the grimoire on to a magickal apprentice.

Your grimoire is as personal to you as the medicine and magick you carry and the proprietary blend you practice. What you decide to put inside is a direct reflection of you and your magick's uniqueness.

THE GRAND LIBRARY

In the land of Spirit, there is a library with never-ending walls and no ceilings, where all the records—of what was, what is, and ever will be—are written in endless volumes of books. Fate and Destiny both dance here with La Muerte as an open invitation guest. Most of the library is packed to the brim with shelves full of books that are written, prewritten, or written by default. Most of us, and our ancestors from eons past, live here.

But there is one shelf, tucked in a corner and hidden in plain sight, where the book's pages are at varying stages of empty. Books where the pages seem to write themselves.

Of all the Grand Library has to offer, this is La Muerte's favorite corner. La Muerte observes the words come to life on their own and watches the pages turn of their own accord. La Muerte witnesses book after book on this special shelf capture a force equally as powerful as La Muerte's own, but one they've never known: The unshakeable, unbreakable, and undeniable force of the Humxn Spirit.

Your Journal as a Grimoire

As a magickal tool for transformation, your grimoire is your personal codex—a book, journal, and diary—of your metamorphosis and becoming. This is a journey you have already begun; with the journal you have kept throughout this book! Your journal, or grimoire, is becoming the book whose pages seem to write themselves—you are writing yourself, your experiences, opportunities, and life into being by becoming a conscious creatrix of it.

The most important and transformative way to work with your grimoire is committing to engage and interact with it daily—and giving yourself the time and space to review and reflect on what you wrote. Your grimoire will speak to you in patterns that can only be recognized if you consistently write things down, track them, and then reflect on them.

You can do this by creating a ritual of review—a specific day of the week, month, or Moon cycle that you devote to reengaging and reviewing the magick you wrote down for that specific time period. As you become consistent with this practice, you'll begin to understand what these patterns mean, how to change them (if you want to), and deepen your relationship with all the resources and support around you— all keys to transforming your life with magick.

Working with Your Grimoire

There is no right or wrong way to work with your grimoire. My grimoire is a modge-podge of magick. It serves as my personal book of days. It is a space that i enter daily, to record the medicine, lessons, and growth of the day. It is my tracker for any manifestations that came to fruition. It logs all the animal, bird, or elemental allies that showed up to support me. By the end of each season, i have a complete, 360-degree record of the magick in my life, how i worked with it (or didn't), and how i utilized the other tools as gateways for my continual and ever-evolving transformation.

PRAXIS: SETTING UP YOUR GRIMOIRE

Your grimoire is also your ride-or-die life and magickal bestie that gives you tough love, offers advice, and a shoulder to cry on whenever you need a secret and safe place to be or vent. In this praxis, you're going to focus on setting up your grimoire to be the most supportive ally to your magick. i'll also share with you some ideas on how to specifically work with your grimoire to assist and guide you in your transformation.

1 If you decide to choose a new grimoire (rather than continue with the journal you chose as your tool at the beginning of this book), now is the time to do it. From a designated folder on your computer to an inexpensive diary, planner, or notebook from the dollar store, the options for your grimoire are endless. Always choose the one that resonates and makes you feel something the most.

2 Set an intention for your grimoire (see Intention, page 56). Create (and do) an anointment ritual. Use this as an opportunity to infuse it with your desire for it to be a guide, aid, and ally in your personal transformation and Wild Dreams.

3 Intentionally write your name on the first page. This creates an immediate bond between you and your grimoire.

4 Decide how you want to section your grimoire—if you want to section it out at all. You can divide your grimoire by New Moon cycles, monthly, seasonally, by tools you're working with—the possibilities are endless. Or you can leave it blank and choose your own adventure as you go.

TRANSFORMATION INSPIRATION FOR WORKING WITH YOUR GRIMOIRE

- Create a log of daily feelings, omens, card pulls, synchronicities, situations, and magick as they relate to the navigation of your transformation.

- Write your Wild Dreams at the front of your grimoire and use the rest of the pages to track your magick spells and inspired actions toward them.

- Scribe your notes, reflections, and emotions as you continue down the path of metamorphosis. Take care to record your magickal and transformational milestones.

- Refer back to the traditional ways to use your grimoire bullet points and implement one (or all) of those approaches.

- Paste leaves from each seasonal cycle, tea or cookie fortune fortunes, napkin drawings, doodles, and downloads from the Universe, receipts from purchases that you made in service to your Wild Dreams—anything big or small that feels like a personal or energetic milestone to you.

- Finally, create your ritual for review. Choose your frequency—weekly, monthly, seasonally, whatever feels best for you—and show up to the magick in your life, consistently.

As we move through the following pages, i offer more opportunities to work with our grimoires in both traditional and innovative ways. For instance, to channel and download magick through Spirit Writing (see page 119), to track animal allies as they present themselves to us (see page 110), and to explore connections between our magick via Intersectional Alchemy (see opposite). Your grimoire can also become your companion and guide for the 30 Days of Magick for Transformation—Your Wild Dream Life Challenge at the end of this book.

Intersectional Alchemy

Intersectionality is Love's gift to us all. It reminds us that separation is an illusion and that everything—and everyone—is connected. It is a new way to understand, engage, and work with your magick—and yourself.

We are all intersectional beings. You are made up of bone, blood, thyroid, cells, body parts, spirit, marrow, organs, skin, a beautiful and magnanimous beating heart, and so many other miraculous things. But you are not any one of those things. You are not even the sum of them.

You/i/we/us spring forth from the magick and science of all these random elements working together, in tandem, and from the places and spaces where all the elements that make us up come together and intersect to create something wholly new and totally alive—you.

THE GIFT OF FIRE

Once there was a Little Spirit who wanted to be born on Earth. Earth said, "Yes, and i give you my soil in the form of flesh to bring your outside to life." Wind said, "Yes, and i give you my thermals in the form of breath to bring your insides to life." Water said, "Yes, and i give you my life sustaining waters in the form of blood to steward all life inside you." Soon Moon, Stars, and Sun showed up to offer Little Spirit their medicine as a parting gift.

Little Spirit gave many thanks to each before turning to face Fire. Fire's flames curled up in a playful smile and said "i've already given you a gift!" Little Spirit felt confused but Fire continued, "i gifted you my spark of initial desire. Where else would your desire to be born come from?" Now Little Spirit was the one smiling.

Fire then blazed into fullness and for the first time, Little Spirit felt scared. But Fire continued, "You may go, Little Spirit.

And i give you my blazing flames in the form of your heart to ignite all the gifts you've been given into your new Earth-bound life." At that exact moment, Little Spirit felt lightning bolt charges inside their newfound body as Fire's heart brought all the other gifts to life and transformed them into Humxn Spirit.

Humxn Spirit opened all their eyes as they felt what being alive feels like for the first time. Excited, Humxn Spirit was about to leap off the precipice that separated the Spirit World from the Earthly World when Love tapped them on their newly formed shoulder and said, "i have one last gift to give—i give you the gifts of relationship, compassion, and interconnectedness in the form of the one thing that connects us all—love." And with that Humxn Spirit and Love leaped to Earth.

What Is Intersectionality?

We are a culmination of things—our culture, our choices, our beliefs, where we live, our nature and nurture, and what media we consume. The results—how we behave, what we believe—doesn't come from any one of these things. It comes from the intersection of them all.

Intersectionality is the basis of all life. A tree is the result of seed. It bisects the soil, comes into contact with Water, consumes Sun, and breaches Earth. The tree becomes a living, breathing representation of the intersection of all those things made flesh.

Intersectionality is where our potential and power are made real. Intersectional Alchemy is about acknowledging that we are inherently intersectional beings and consciously using that knowledge to see the interconnectedness of all things—our magick and transformation included. When we begin to see ourselves, not as parts, but as something grand that is birthed when all our parts come together, then we are truly living from our limitless potential.

INTERSECTIONAL ALCHEMY AND THE TAROT

Because Intersectional Alchemy is a unique form of magick gifted to me by Spirit, i want to give you a tangible example to help you understand what it looks like in magick.

The Western esoteric and occult group of the Hermetic Order of the Golden Dawn was the first magickal collective to bridge tarot with astrology and the Kabbalah. This created a new, deeply layered, intersectional meaning for each card. Each card became a vessel and gateway to a plethora of occult and mystical teachings, from the twelve signs of the zodiac and their decans, the planets, to the ten Sephiroth on Kabbalah's Tree of Life.

So, when we pull a card, we are reading all these elements—astrology, decans, the Sephiroth—all together. The meaning we make (alchemy) comes from the center where all these occult teachings meet, i.e. the intersection of them all.

Practicing Intersectional Alchemy

There are three steps to incorporating Intersectional Alchemy in your own life.

Connect (Intersectionality): drawing, making, and seeing the connections that are already there.

Integrate (Alchemy): recognize the truth that we are connected to everything and everything is connected to us. When we do this, we open ourselves up to unexpected assistance, ideas, and advice from magick itself.

Expand (Intersectional Alchemy): embody this newfound wisdom in our lives.

PRAXIS: WEB OF INTERSECTIONS

In this praxis, i will walk you through the three steps to practicing Intersectional Alchemy. Once you learn these three elements, you can then replicate the results you get in this praxis with anything else in your life. Once you have your answers from step 3, take action!

1 Connection (intersectionality): Let's use today's day of the week as our Intersectional Alchemy starting point. So, if you're reading this book on a Sunday, write "Sunday" down in your grimoire. Start listing all the magickal connections that correspond to Sunday. You can take this step as deep as you want. Feel free to do some research if you have to. The goal of this step is to build a bank of things that connect and relate to your starting point.

For example, here are some connections i would observe:

- The Sun, center of our solar system

- The Sun tarot card

- The astrological sign of Leo

- Sunday is the first day of the week (Number one relates to new beginnings and leadership in numerology)

- The first house in astrology rules the self (Aries corresponds to the first house, the Emperor is Aries tarot card)

2 Integrate (alchemy): Look at how some (or all!) of the connections you listed in step 2 relate to you and your life. Pay attention to any aha! moments (or Light Rabbits, see page 70), answers to questions we have, or any other pertinent information or support you need. There is so much medicine in that discovery alone so enjoy your time and stay open to any magick that you find. For example, here are some questions i would ask:

- Where does Leo sit in my chart?

- When was the last time i pulled The Sun tarot card? What was going on in my life then?

- Are there any current transits happening in my 5th house (the house that Leo rules)?

- Where in my life am i feeling like a beginner right now?

- Is there something in my life that i need to see with a beginner's mind?

- Where do i need to take a more leadership role in my life?

3 Expand (intersectional alchemy): Explore how you can embody this newfound wisdom in your life and expand this medicine out to the world. Here are some questions that can help you bridge the gap:

- How can i implement this medicine in my life?

- What is one action i can take (or something i could do differently) based on this information?

- How can i use what i learned to better serve my clients, my friends, my partner, and myself?

- What has this Intersectional Alchemy experience taught me about how i want to relate to the world?

XIX THE SUN

Medicine Wheel

The Medicine Wheel is a cyclical way to understand and work with the natural world around you. To learn who you are—and who you are becoming.

The Wheel of Life, Medicine Wheel, Wheel of the Year—there are as many variations of Medicine Wheel as there are names to call it. Your culture, lineage, and/or spiritual heritage and beliefs will define what direction and allies each quadrant of the Wheel represents.

i work with the Aztec Medicine Wheel, as this Wheel is Mother to my ancestor's medicine and native to my soul. But it is radically different in its correspondences from other Wheels (for example, which season relates to which direction, and so on). However, because all my work (including this book) is based on and in the Aztec Medicine Wheel, i want to introduce you to its particular medicine blend.

In Medicine Wheel, each direction is associated with a season, element, color, animal ally, period of life, and a specific deity. When we work with Medicine Wheel as a transformational tool (which you'll do next), we are engaging holistically with the totality of where and how all these mystical components that make it up intersect with each other.

THE DIRECTIONS OF THE AZTEC MEDICINE WHEEL

TLĀHUIZLĀMPA (EAST)
Season: Spring
Element: Fire (Huehuetéotl)
Color: Red
Deity: Xīpe Totēc
Animal Ally/Symbol: Quail
Period of Life: Child

HUĪTZLĀMPA (SOUTH)
Season: Summer
Element: Water (Tlāloc)
Color: Blue
Deity: Huītzilopōchtli
Animal Ally/Symbol: Hummingbird
Period of Life: Adolescent/Student

CIHUATLĀMPA (WEST)
Season: Autumn
Element: Earth (Tlāltēcuhtli)
Color: White
Deity: Quetzalcohuātl
Animal Ally/Symbol: Feathered Serpent
Period of Life: Adult/Teacher

MICTLĀMPA (NORTH)
Season: Winter
Element: Air/Wind (Ehēcatl)
Color: Black
Deity: Tezcatlipōca
Animal Ally/Symbol: Black Jaguar
Period of Life: Elder/Wisest of Teachers

THE FOUR DIRECTIONS

In the beginning, Earth was covered in an infinite ocean. At night, the ocean waters would spring forth from North, East, South, and West, tower over each direction, and meet in the center of Midnight's sky.

In these waters lived the greatest sea monster that ever was. Quetzalcohuātl and his brother, Tēzcatlipōca, battled the monster for seven nights until, finally, victory was theirs. As sea monster's blood returned to the waters that birthed it, the vast ocean covering Earth receded. As the water lowered, the brothers created Sky and Earth.

As the waters retreated they spilled into Earth's caves, fertilizing the soil and gifting all creatures with nutrients to sustain and grow life. As the waters withdrew into Earth's lakes, rivers, and oceans, five cosmic colossal trees grew in their stead to ensure Sky would not collapse. Four in each of the directions from which the ocean spouted and the fifth in the center of Earth. Thus, Medicine Wheel was formed and magick would soon follow suit.

The Fifth Direction

On the previous page (see page 98) are the directional, elemental, and ally correspondences for the Aztec Medicine Wheel. The fifth direction is the center of the Wheel, the place where all the components—the seasons and elements, their associated colors, deities, and allies, and you—intersect. This center is known as the heart of the world and illustrates how every component of your world comes to life. In the following praxis, you'll learn how to work with all the components of the Aztec Medicine Wheel.

PRAXIS: A SEASON OF THE WHEEL

In this praxis, we are working with Medicine Wheel to help us see how much we transform, shift, and change in a season—just like all the nature around us. You will need your grimoire and a pen, your Index Card of Wild Dreams (see page 42), and your tarot or oracle deck.

1 Let's start with whatever season you are currently in. Whether you're at the beginning of the season or the end, take a moment to acknowledge where you are in the cycle and devote a section for it in your grimoire.

2 Choose a Wild Dream to pursue during this season—pick one from your Index Card of Wild Dreams.

3 Pull a guiding card. Get your body into a comfortable position, thumb through your deck, and pick a card. Now, set a timer for 10 minutes and journal in your grimoire about how this card relates to you and your Wild Dreams.

4 Now invite all your senses to the party (if you need a refresher, revisit Sensing, page 71). The Wheel shifts subtly but when you open yourself up to the world around you, magick reveals itself to you. Take some time to journal what you're sensing in the season:

- What birds are you hearing?

- What animals (if any) are you seeing?

- What does the temperature outside feel like in your body?

- How does the air taste and/or feel on your skin?

- What do you see?

- What energies can you sense?

5 Now that you've situated yourself within the season, return to the Medicine Wheel (see page 98) and its correspondences. Begin to reflect on how these elements might connect to you. Perhaps research the deity and animal ally of the season and see if, when, and where the animal shows up. Add the color of the season to something that you're wearing. Practice Intersectional Alchemy (see page 93)—use the element or season as a starting point, build your connections out, and circle them back to you.

6 At the end of the season, take a moment to reflect on what the season brought you.

7 You might choose to continue the praxis over the next season. If you carry out this praxis over a full Medicine Wheel cycle, you'll have a catalog and invaluable resource for your magick that you can refer back to again and again!

Moon Magick

Of all the elements, Moon is our most natural ally and guide to our transformation. Renewing and releasing, reflection and introspection, and beginning and endings are all inherent in the Moon's natural 29-day cycle.

Since the dawn of time, Moon has held the humxn spirit captive. We've sung nursery rhymes about a man coming down from it and cows jumping over it, woven tales that it was made of cheese, wished it Goodnight, and penned many a poem to, for, and about it. We've worshiped her and then been demonized for it. We've built spaceships to both occupy and catch a glimpse of her. But very few of us take the time to really understand her.

In magick, Moon is one of our most versatile allies. When she is new, we can work with her to set our intentions for the coming weeks, and when she is full, we celebrate those intentions coming to fruition. We charge our crystals, make Moon water, and gather in womxn circles (a collective of spiritual and witchy femme-identifying folxs) to commune with Moon. In astrology, we work with our Moon signs to understand our emotions, cravings, and the soul's experience within its humxn body. In tarot, The Moon card references the underbelly, the shadow side, and secrets.

Moon holds many mysteries—but a deep and focused exploration of any one of the modalities in Moon's traditional usage can and will reveal so much about yourself to yourself.

RABBIT MOON

Many Moons ago, before Moon was as we know her today, Quetzalcohuātl transformed himself from a God to humxn and walked among us. As a God in newly humxn form, he soon found himself growing tired and hungry. Weary under the heat of his own creation, Sun, he stopped in the middle of a lush green grove to rest, his hunger pains exceeding anything he had ever felt or known.

Quetzalcohuātl noticed Rabbit munching on grass. As their eyes met, Rabbit spoke, "Hello, humxn kin. May i ask what is wrong with you?" Quetzalcohuātl replied, "Nilzē, Rabbit. i'm tired and very hungry." Rabbit offered their new humxn companion a handful of grass. "Tlazocamati," Quetzalcohuātl replied in genuine gratitude, "but what nourishes and fills your belly will not do the same for mine." "What will you do?" Rabbit asked. Quetzalcohuātl grew desolate and grim as he remembered the humxn cycle he created. "Die," the Great God said.

Rabbit thought for a moment, then with conviction and pride, said, "i am but a small creature, but i know i can help." They stepped closer to their new friend and said, "i'm here. Eat me."

Quetzalcohuātl was stunned silent by Rabbit's kindness and sacrifice. He scooped Rabbit up in his hand and revealed his true form. Rabbit's eyes grew big and wide in recognition of the Feathered Serpent God.

Up, up, up they went through the cosmos until Quetzalcohuātl reached Moon. He turned to his brave friend and said, "For your courage, i gift you Moon" and cast Rabbit's shadow onto Moon. "Moon will forever hold your tale of kindness to me. And your kindness will live on as you cast your goodwill in tandem with the light of Moon. You and Moon are now one. Together you will be known as Moon Rabbit." With that, Quetzalcohuātl returned Rabbit to their patch.

Working with Moon Magick

Moon magick for transformation cycles back to four of the eight skills shared earlier in this book—Energy (see page 51), Intention (see page 56), Congruency (see page 78), and Self-leadership (see page 84).

The energy and intentionality we bring to our Moon work directly dictate and impact the direction our focus will flow. The way we draw down that intentionality and energy into our daily lives, and live it out through our behaviors, actions, and choices, is directly proportional to how congruent and committed we are to hold ourselves accountable (self-leadership) to what we say we are going to do.

The beauty of working with Moon is her reassurance that we do not have to go at it alone. When we work with Moon for our personal transformation, we are doing so in divine connection and lineage of our ancestors.

PRAXIS: BUILDING DEEPER CONNECTIONS

Oftentimes when we are working with Moon via our New Moon intentions, we are doing so in a two-dimensional way—on pen and paper. But Moon is alive! And basking in her energy, fullness, and shadows is a completely different experience. This is why, for this praxis, i'm going to ask you to relate to Moon in a more embodied way. Put away your Moon app, grab your grimoire and a pen, and just sit with Moon as she is. This is the kind of deep relationship Moon wants us to cultivate, not just with her, but will all our magickal tools, elements, and Earth.

1 Go outside, wherever you need to find Moon in the night sky. Once you find her, make a note of where you are in your grimoire, so you can return to this place.

2 For the next 20 minutes or so, i want you to gaze at Moon and feel her. Remember the sensing skills (see page 71) you practiced earlier in the book? Return to it. Really see and sense her. Challenge yourself to move beyond your sensory comfort zone and the ways you would traditionally interact and work with Moon.

3 Take out your grimoire but try not to write what you're feeling. Sketch or doodle it out. Sketch whatever phase she's in and any aspects of Rabbit you can see. Sketch what you hear, smell, and taste under this Moon. Shade in the shadows. If you feel called to write, see if you can describe whatever it is in a limerick or poem. If physical sight is not accessible to you, enter your relationship with Moon via whatever sense is.

4 Repeat steps 1–3 for the next 30 nights. As you move throughout the 30 days, look up and see if you can find my favorite Moon of all—Day Moon. This is when Moon shows up in the day sky. If she does, spend some time sketching and sensing Day Moon too.

5 When your 30 days are done, pull out your Personal Energy Map (see page 54). See if you can align your sketches with the notes from that praxis. From the feelings and emotions you wrote down back then to the sketches and doodles you sense now, spend some time taking in the totality of your relationship with Moon.

Energy Work

Whenever i introduce energy work to folxs, i always liken it to Wind. Energy, like Wind, is not a force we can physically see with our eyes; we can only experience it once it arrives—like the blowing of the trees—or when we're caught in a whirlwind of it.

The movement of energy is much like that of Wind—it can vary in degrees from subtle to destructive, it can roam and rage free, or it can be conjured and contained. So, as you move through the following pages, i want you to think about energy like Wind and "work" as the manipulation of it.

THE GIFT OF WIND

Ehēcatl, God of Wind, created the breath of all life with a tap of his finger. As Earth and their inhabitants—Rabbit, Hummingbird, Jaguar, Oak, Wolf, Bee, and all other creatures—stood still and lifeless, Ehēcatl focused on them and said, "Now i shall breathe life into all of you."

As his last word was spoken, Winds numbering billions gathered, gushed, and swirled around all of Earth's inhabitants. Once all Winds were in place in front of their respective creature, Ehēcatl, with a flick of his beak, gave the order for Winds to enter each one through their heart space, bringing all things to life. What was once a still life, became alive.

Calling back all Winds, Ehēcatl turned to the remains of the Third and Fourth Suns and from their ashes created you and me. He then gifted us Wind, the element we cannot see, as a reminder that the energy and air that animates all things is the same force breathing in and flowing out through the heart of you.

Pushing the Boundaries of What Is Possible

Anything that moves, shifts, and helps us unblock the flow of energy inside and outside our bodies is energy work. Energy Work can be experienced in a variety of ways, for example, through reiki, qigong, tai chi, and mudras (see Glossary, page 140). Dancing, meditation, breathwork, and tapping (because it moves energy through and out of us), are also forms of energy work.

Often when we think about transformation, we start by shifting things that are outside of us, because it's easy to change our looks, habits, environment, house, or body. We've all heard the stories of people who have won the lotto, became millionaires overnight, and then burned through their money in a year. This happens because while their external situation changed (for example, an increase in money), their inner world—their energy, mindset, and beliefs—stayed the same.

Transformation requires us to dig deeper and shift the things we cannot see. This is much harder. Energy work shifts our inner world, and in doing so, creates more space in our environment. Think about those times you felt you outgrew something, so you got rid of it. The release (and therefore the space) happened because something (your energy) shifted inside you first. This then made it easy to let go of the thing because you had already energetically grown beyond it.

Energy work is vital to our transformation work. When we use energy work as a tool for transformation, we are manipulating energy to help us be our most powerful, full, and attuned selves.

PRAXIS: CALLING BACK YOUR POWER

Have you found your body's energy centers? Many people feel a power center near the base of their bellies where the lower dantian and sacral chakra are located. Some feel it in their heart center, others in their throat, or upper arms, and so on. If you have not yet done the praxis Body Energy Centers (see page 55), flip back and complete that first. The following steps build upon the energy center(s) you've found. This is one of the most powerful exercises you can do for yourself because it directly influences your mood, feelings, and ultimately your actions.

1 Choose the energy center that feels like your personal center of power, where your unique energy, medicine, and strength come from and through.

2 Close your eyes and imagine a huge magnet residing in your chosen power center.

3 Imagine your energy center magnetizing all the pieces and parts of you back into your body—the you that made breakfast this morning, the you who is still reeling from a bad decision you made over a decade ago, the you who has yet to heal from a certain heartbreak, the you of last night, and the you of the moment before you began this praxis. The goal of this step is to plug energy leaks. Call your power back from all the places, experiences, sources, and versions of you, so you can feel fully present (and fully YOU) in this moment, right here.

4 Continue calling yourself back to yourself until you feel "full." When we are new to this practice, our energetic system can get overwhelmed since we're not used to holding so much of ourselves inside our energetic body. This can create a bloating and almost nauseous feeling—like the way we feel when we overeat—because we're asking our energetic system to stretch far beyond what it's used to.

5 Open your eyes. In your grimoire, make a note of any bodily sensations you're feeling and the parts of yourself you've called back in.

6 Commit to doing this praxis daily. In your grimoire, keep tabs on how much energy your system can hold and how being fully in yourself affects the big and small things in your life. As you continue to practice daily, you will find that your capacity for what you can hold expands.

Ancestors and Animal Allies

We are all born with a pantheon of ancestors and spirit and animal allies. However, most of us—including myself—weren't raised in cultures or home environments that cultivated this awareness and connection to all the support, medicine, and magick we are born with. We have to seek out these connections ourselves.

The most accessible place to start when you're trying to reconnect to your pantheon is with the ancestors that are closest to you—your blood relations. Your blood ancestors are your humxn-form ancestors like your grandmother, great-grandfather, and on down the line.

THE GOLDEN TEARDROP

When you decided to be birthed into being, the Universe wept a single tear. As their golden teardrop fell upon Earth, it landed in the exact place, at the exact time, on the exact humxn you would be birthed through.

You were ushered through Universe's birthing channel on streams and clusters of constellations and epochs of shooting stars. You were surrounded in the womb by Praying Mantises, Deers, Vultures, and Wolves. You were nurtured to bloom and chosen by the animal whose destiny would be bound to you—and you forever to it.

Wrapped in your tona's medicine, you were carried through Earth's belly and through your humxn's womb on the shoulders and backs of all your ancestors that came before you. You would always be a part of them—and they of you.

While humxn ancestors are those that most of us are familiar with, our ancestral allies also include the lands in which your ancestors were born. We all originate somewhere beyond where modern geography tells us, and the lands where your story began are part of your blood ancestral lineage too.

You are made up of spirit and soul, and so you also have what i call your spiritual kin—those ancestors that resonate and relate to your spirit. These can show up at any point in your life and may be animals or people who've passed that you don't personally know (like songwriters, poets, authors, artists), particular places, and elements that inexplicably move your soul.

Calling Your Allies

As in the story of The Golden Teardrop (see opposite), you also have spirit and animal allies that have been with you since birth. In my culture, we believe that a specific animal ally with whom you are deeply connected, and whose destiny is intricately linked to your own, grows with you in the womb. This animal ally is called your tona (or animal tona). They are born into the world with you and stay with you throughout the entire course of your life. They serve as a guide, omen, talisman, or whatever else you need, at the exact moment you need it.

Check in with yourself to see if you already know what your animal tona is—i know i did. i knew because it was the animal that was present and constantly showing up at different times in my life. i knew because i felt a deep, unexplainable connection to it. i knew it because i sensed it—and i trusted what i intuitively and psychically knew. If you're still not sure, try the guided journey (below) to help you discover it.

Along with your animal tona, your blood ancestors, and your spiritual kin, you also have allies you were born into based on your birth chart and the season and day you were born on/in. These natal allies include, but are not limited to, your elemental, planetary, day of the week, and zodiac allies.

Building Your Pantheon

One of the most important components of magick and transformation work is your spirit team—what i call your pantheon. When we assemble and work with our ancestors, animal allies, and spirit guides, we do so from a rich and intersectionally holistic approach. In the following praxis, i'm going to guide you through finding two members of your spiritual support team—one natal ally and your tona (born ally).

PRAXIS: YOUR TONA

If you already know what your tona (born-with animal ally) is, write it down in your grimoire. Start to consciously create a relationship with it (see step 10). If you're still not sure, try the steps below.

The one question i get asked the most when i take my flients through this praxis is: "How do i know for sure that i have the right tona?" My answer is always the same. You'll know. You'll know because it will all start to make sense—how your life has unfolded, why you were drawn to certain colors or textures, and so on—like random pieces of torn paper coming together to form a pattern in a collage. Trust it.

1 Find a quiet, comfortable place where you can be undisturbed for 5-10 minutes. Close your eyes and take three deep breaths.

2 Ride your next inhale into your body. Drop your awareness into your heart and belly-button space. As you exhale, ride your breath back up. As you continue to breathe, begin to build an energetic bridge between your heart center and your belly button. When the connection feels solid, release the building energy, and expand your awareness into that space.

3 Now bring into your energy field all the animals, insects, birds, and reptiles you can think of. Sit with the collective animal energy field for some breaths. Say hello and give thanks for all their medicine and gifts they bestow upon you/i/we/us.

4 As you continue to swirl in their energies, ask the animal who knew you and was with you in the womb to come forward.

5 If one creature comes forward, spend time in its energy. Do you feel any particular sensations? Check in with the bridge between your heart and belly button. Remember your tona was in the womb with you so you should feel some kind of energetic connection in or around your belly button—the place on your body that forever links you/i/we/us back to the womb.

6 If more than one creature comes forward, repeat step 5 with each one. Does your heart space flutter more when a certain creature comes forward? What about your belly button? Do you feel any sensations arising from there?

7 If nothing comes forward, that's okay too. Sometimes we have to do this praxis a couple of times—especially if we don't already have a solid kinship with animals. Trust must be built. Repeat steps 1–4 again in a few days and pay attention to any creatures that present themselves to you in the physical world between now and then.

8 Thank all the creatures for their presence. Ride your breath back into your body and back into your physical space.

9 In your grimoire, journal everything that came through during your session.

10 In the upcoming weeks, spend some time with the creature who came forward. Start to consciously create a relationship with it. Learn its qualities, energies, and medicine. Do an Intersectional Alchemy session (see page 93) to discover the universe it connects you to. Your goal is to build a solid and ever-evolving relationship. Show up for your tona and it will do the same for you.

PRAXIS: YOUR ELEMENTAL ALLY

This element became your ally the second you were born and is a member of your natal allies. We'll be using your birth chart to find them. You'll need to know your date, time, and place of birth. If you don't know your exact time of birth, use noon (or check the "unknown time" button if you're using astro-seek.com), but remember this won't be the most accurate reflection of your birth chart.

1 Enter your birth information here: horoscopes.astro-seek.com/calculate-birth-chart-horoscope-online

2 Click on "Extended settings: House Systems, Aspects, Orbs" and for House System choose "Whole Sign" from the drop-down menu.

3 Click the "Calculate Chart" button.

4 Once you're redirected to your birth chart, you'll see six tabs. Navigate to the final tab labeled "Dominants" and click it. The element that is most dominant in your birth chart is your natal elemental ally— and if you have two elements that are equally dominant, then you have two allies!

5 Now that you have another member of your pantheon, take some time to get to know it, as you have with your tona (see step 10, page 113).

Tarot

Tarot as a magickal tool is far too expansive to include everything about it in one book. On the following pages, i offer you an introduction to help jump-start your relationship with it and to work with it as a magickal tool for transformation.

Tarot is my favorite tool of magick and my go-to for guidance on transformation. i started my relationship with tarot in my 20s, got serious with it in early 2020, and we took our relationship to the next level when tarot became the impetus and inspiration for Intersectional Alchemy.

TAROT: AN INTERSECTIONAL ALCHEMY ORIGIN STORY

Great Spirit loved their humxn creation so much and wished for a way to commune with them through space and time. So Great Spirit called the first Grand Meeting of All Deities, spanning cultures and millennials to share this desire.

Immediately, Oshun gave birth to the idea of symbols on papyrus they could hold in their hands. Quan Yin infused them with humxn soul's plight and the journey of enlightenment, and Shiva created them into a deck of cards. The four Aztec Gods of Wind, Fire, Water, and Earth infused their medicine into symbols on the cards that humxns could understand—Ehēcatl's Wind as swords, Huehuetéotl's Fire as Wands, Tlāloc's Water as Cups, and Tlāltēcuhtli's Earth as Coins.

Each of the Supreme Beings present added a molecule of their medicine to each of the cards, bringing the Spirit of the cards to life. Thoth wove all the wisdom and energy of the ancients together, numbered each card, and sprinkled the entire deck with mysticism and magick. Thunderbird carried the cards from the world of spirit to the land of Earth, and delivered them to Ether, who then shrouded the origin of the cards in a blanket of mystery.

Tarot was born. As was humxn's direct line to commune with Great Spirit and all things Divine.

A Brief Introduction to Tarot

In each deck, 22 cards (numbered 0–21) make up the Major Arcana. The Major Arcana cards, also known as the big secrets, traditionally represent the humxn experience—the big milestones and lessons we encounter in life and how to move through them.

The other 56 cards in the deck make up the Minor Arcana, or lesser secrets, which traditionally represent the ins and outs of daily life. The Minor Arcana is broken into four suits (Wands, Cups, Swords, and Pentacles) with each suit numbered from ace to ten, plus a Page, Knight, Queen, and King. These court cards—16 in total—traditionally have multiple meanings and could represent you, someone else, or a situation in your life.

Tarot for Transformation

As magick for transformation practitioners, we use tarot in much the same way as traditional folxs. The major difference is that we come to the cards with the energy (see page 51), intention (see page 56), and mindset (see page 62) of transformation. We bring the desire (energy) for transformation and the cards show us how to make it happen.

The 22 Major Arcana become your archetypical guides. They are the gateway (your intersectional alchemy) into the spirit, energetics, and story of your transformation. They represent big spiritual and energetic shifts that are needed (or are happening) in your current transformational journey.

The 56 Minor Arcana represent how to embody the spiritual and intersectional alchemy learnings in your life. They reveal the practical behaviors, habits, and changes needed to make your manifestations real. The 16 court cards become the stages of transformation you are either in right now, are venturing to become, or the energy of who you need to be to make your transformation a reality.

Each card provides a metaphysical glimpse as to how we can holistically embody our Wild Dreams—and who we need

to step into to make them come true. Every daily draw, every spread, every question asked and answered, becomes a potential portal of personal transformation. Every time you draw a card, every card you receive, can be—and is—life-changing. This is real, big magick. This is you fully stepping into your power and approaching tarot as a vehicle to create radical and lasting change in your life.

Some of the more traditional ways that folxs work with tarot cards include themed spreads, questions and answers, daily card pulls, and readings for themselves or others. There are so many ways to work with tarot to aid your transformation, the possibilities are endless. In the following praxis, i'll share two of my favorites.

PRAXIS: YOUR TRANSFORMATION DECK

Choose a specific deck to be your "Transformation Deck." This will be the deck you use anytime you want to work with tarot to help guide and advise you on your transformation journey.

1 Hold each of your decks in your hands and sense what it wants to say. Choose the one that speaks and feels transformative to you.

2 Ask the deck if it wants to be your deck of transformation simply by shuffling the cards and asking it. The card you receive will be your answer.

3 Once you have received a positive answer from one of your decks, anoint it as your deck of transformations. Simply state out loud that it is so—and so shall it be. You could also create your own ceremony to infuse it with your energy of transformation.

4 After you've anointed it, do not use it for any other kind of readings or questions. This helps keep the energy of the deck crystal clear and your readings more potent.

PRAXIS: YOUR PERSONALIZED SPREAD FOR TRANSFORMATION

Use your anointed-for-transformation deck (see page 117) to create this personalized spread for transformation. Follow the below steps with the tarot card you pulled as Your Archetype Card (see page 33). In this example, i used Nine of Pentacles.

1 Get clear on what you want to know and then form your desire into a themed topic. For example, How can i welcome the abundance of the Nine of Pentacles in my life?

2 Write down all the questions you have about this topic.

- What did the womxn in the card have to believe to get to her garden of abundance?

- What actions can i take to embody this card?

- What are some of the habits and boundaries that somebody like the Nine of Pentacles might have?

3 Write down all the pieces of information that would be helpful to you about this topic.

- What obstacles should the Nine of Pentacles watch out for?

- What kind of mindset does the womxn in the Nine of Pentacles have?

- How does she spend her time?

4 Leave room for magick by adding in some questions that invite Spirit and spontaneity in.

- What allies want to support me in this journey?

- What message does the Nine of Pentacles have for me?

- What does Spirit want me to know?

5 Once you have a list of questions, choose a mix that gives you the most complete picture of your topic. Sense into which questions want to be answered, and try to include one from each of the three sections.

6 Finally, arrange the questions in an order that feels good to you. Pay attention to any shapes that organically come through (if nothing does, lines and rows work just as magickally!) i arranged my cards with the Nine of Pentacles at the top, then three rows of cards in a pyramid shape underneath.

Spirit Writing

Do you ever have a moment when you write something, and afterwards, you look it over and wonder "Where did that come from?" That is Spirit guiding your words and/or writing.

Spirit Writing is writing from the soul that channels the Divine. It's the practice of letting go—getting your ego, inner critic, self-doubt, and overthinking out of the way. When we remove our conscious need for control, we open up space to sense our answers and channel them from the Universe, through our body, and out of our hands. Spirit Writing allows you to birth your brilliance, amplify your voice, and be a clear channel for Spirit.

STREAM OF CONSCIOUSNESS

In the center of the Universe, there is an infinite, ever-flowing stream full of the waters of consciousness, the raging of ideas, and whirlpools of stories and words.

Around 1500BCE, Egyptians dipped into that stream to scribe The Book of the Dead. In 868BCE, The Diamond Sutra was birthed to Buddhists from the heart of that stream. Between 400BCE and 200BCE, the great sage Vyasa embodied the stream to author The Bhagavad Gita. Between 1021 and 1154CE, the Mayans channeled the stream in their oldest codex, Códice Maya de México. The

Torah, Bible, Sutras, and all other great books, ideas, and innovations originate from this stream.

The heart of the Universe cracked open, making room for each and every one of us to tap into their consciousness and channel it out. One stream. So many stories. It's time to channel yours.

The Three Forms of Spirit Writing

As we navigate our transformation, Spirit Writing as a tool gives us direct access to advice and next steps we need to take. It also strengthens our relationships with Spirit and our intuition through the medium of writing and vehicle of channeling. The three forms of spirit writing we will work with in magick for transformation are:

Freewriting: The goal of freewriting is to bypass your brain and tap into your inner guide and Spirit. The way we condition ourselves to do that is by setting a timer and keeping our hand moving for a specific amount of time. As you write, don't stop to think, or go back and edit a misspelled word— stay as radically present as you can.

Automatic Writing: Also known as psychography and intuitive writing, automatic writing is the psychic practice of writing words without thinking about it. Here Spirit moves you, your thoughts, and your hands to write through you.

Channeled Writing: Often called "downloads," this is a form of writing where you show up on a blank page and sense what wants to come through. For example, whenever i'm writing, i hear sentences, phrases, and concepts and then do my best to draw them down, through me, and out of my fingertips.

In the following praxis, we will be trying out all three forms of Spirit Writing over three consecutive days. All three of these praxis are meant to be done over and over again—the more you work with them, the more they will show up and work for you. After three days, or when you feel you've had enough space from them, you can go back and read what you wrote—without judgment and always with a loving, open heart.

PRAXIS: DAY 1: FREEWRITING

1 Grab your grimoire and open to a new page. Set a timer for seven minutes.

2 Choose one of the prompts below and start writing. Focus on keeping your hand moving!

- i remember ...

- i don't remember ...

- i need to remember ...

- i don't want to remember ...

3 When the timer goes off, stop, and close your notebook.

4 Do not read what you wrote, but before you end the session, ask yourself how this praxis made you feel.

PRAXIS: DAY 2: AUTOMATIC WRITING

1 On a new page in your grimoire, write down a question you have or a topic you are currently curious about. You could say something like:

- What do i need to know about today?

- What messages do you want to share with me about [a particular situation you are going through]?

- Please help me practice automatic writing.

2 With pen in hand, close your eyes, take a few deep breaths, and center your energy back into yourself.

3 Hold your question in your energy—really feel it in your body, surrounding you, and pulsating through you. As the energy of your question vibrates around you, place the pen on the paper, and allow your hand to be swept up in its energy. Keep your eyes closed and your mind focused on the question as you allow your hand to move. Stay in the space for as long as you feel something coming through and/or moving your hand.

4 When you feel complete, stop.

5 Do not read what you wrote, but before you end the session, ask yourself how this praxis made you feel.

PRAXIS: DAY 3: CHANNEL WRITING

For this praxis, you have the option to use either pen and paper or your computer. i have found channeled writing easiest when i'm typing—there's something melodic about the sound of a keyboard that opens up a trance-like state of reception in me. Maybe try it on paper first and then again on your computer. You can set a timer, or not—again, i'd try it both ways. This praxis will become easier the more you do it and keep putting yourself in the path of Spirit to speak to you.

1 Shake out your body, then center yourself with your breath. Maybe even do a short meditation to clear and open your mind.

2 Open to a new page or document, and then, pen or fingertips ready ... wait.

3 While you're waiting, i want you to expand your energy and sensing antennas. Open up your entire body—energetic, sensory, mental, all of it—to receive. If nothing appears to be happening for you, stay in the experience! Stay open to receiving words, phrases, and sentences via the portals of all your senses.

4 If or when you sense something, write/type it down. Sometimes the downloads will come barreling through all at once. Other times it's a slow trickle of a word here and sentence there. Your job is to remain present and ready to go when the Divine does speak to you. Trust the process and in your ability to be a channel for Spirit—because you are.

5 Continue to be in a state of receptivity until you feel complete, or until your timer goes off. If you wrote something down, do not read what you wrote, but before you end the session, ask yourself how this praxis made you feel.

Cosmology of You

You are your own cosmology—the origin, development, and ever-evolving theory of an entire universe made up of all things you. You are bundles of stars, balls of energies, a channeler, conjurer, and creatrix of galaxies and multi-dimensional experiences.

You are your own Universe and within you is an entire cosmos and cosmology—a unified whole and your own field of study that brings together all the elements that make you, you.

Like the cosmos itself, you are made up of so many things that taken apart can be overwhelming, but when weaved and understood together can help you see yourself and your life more completely and holistically. Cosmology of You helps you/i/we/us do that.

Become the Center of Your Universe

Cosmology of You is a branch of Intersectional Alchemy (see page 93) that brings together all your metaphysical aspects and cosmic make up so you can know yourself more deeply, alchemize your experiences more completely, and express yourself more fully—in and out of your magick.

Think about it this way: As humxns, we have created an entire field of study called genetics, which helps us to understand the physicality of our being. Our heredity and genetic makeup influences our development, health, who we are, and our lives. In other words, we study how our genes make us who we are. But our genes are only one small piece of our "who we are" story. We are not just humxn flesh and bones made up of the DNA of our genes. We are also Spirit. We also have a soul. We have elements of our self that can't be explained away by logic-centered science.

In the Cosmology of You, we look at all the spiritual, metaphysical, and magickal elements that make us who

we are. From your animal and seasonal allies, numerology, tarot cards, astrological signs, birth chart, and pretty much every tool you've been working on thus far, we can get to know ourselves as whole and complete beings. You are the power source of your magick. And the more profoundly you know yourself, the more potent your magick will be.

In the following praxis, i'm going to help you create a Cosmology of You chart—a collection of all your spiritual and metaphysical makeup that will help you to see the totality of magick you are. Think of Cosmology of You like metaphysical genetics and your chart as your energetic DNA—your soul's cosmic blueprint and your spiritual fingerprint. Being able to fully get to know and understand ourselves in this way unlocks a powerhouse of potentiality and an opportunity to see, access, and express our cosmic power more thoroughly.

PRAXIS: YOUR BASE-LEVEL CHART

Your chart is a complex, soul document—it is way more extensive than anything i can share in this book. However, your base-level chart will give you plenty of information to jump start your Cosmology of You studies and help you begin to see why knowing yourself in this way is important.

1 Head over to Resources (see page 141) for the link to download your free Cosmology of You workbook and video tutorial.

2 The instructions for this praxis are substantial and the online course includes:

- Your Astrological makeup.

- Numerology (including your Life Path number and more).

- Your Tarot Print.

3 In the video and workbook, i walk you through how to create your own Cosmology of You chart step-by-step, plus offer suggestions on how you can begin to integrate your chart into your life.

A GALAXY OF DREAMS

On the day each of us was born, Universe gifted itself in the form of an entire cosmos being birthed inside you/i/we/us. To each was given the agency of the stars, the power of supernovas, and the creatrix/destroyer capacity of Sun. Inside our marrow, carried in our red blood cells and forged in our veins, is the culmination of every Creation story ever written or told. In our ever-unfolding lives and every decision we decide, lies the fates of every God and Goddexx known and unknown. And in the cadence of each heartbeat, woven within threads of every single word said, lies ever-evolving galaxies created each time we say yes to living our Wild Dream Life.

PART III:

Transforming Your Life

As we move into completion of our transformation by alchemizing the learning and medicine of our journey, we call in from the Aztec Medicine Wheel (see page 98) the element of Fire, the direction of Tlāhuizlāmpa (East), and their animal ally of Quail to help you transmute the lessons into your becoming, birthing the Firestarter (changemaker) you were born to be. And so it is.

Thank you. Thank you. Thank you.

Weaving It All Together

Emerging from the land of secrets
You enter into the realm of conscious creator
Birthing bounties of gifts
And the power to make them flesh.
Now Priestess and Empress you're ready to reign,
bringing all worlds together, and
becoming the Emperor and steward
of your Sacred Flame.

Let the Final Magick Begin!

In this alchemical section, you'll weave together everything you've praxised and learned to usher in a new age where you are the sovereign Sacred Creatrix and Emperor of your life. You have come so far. Done so much. You have your knapsack. You've leaped. You garnered new skillsets and polished your tools. You've met your Wild Dreams, channeled your magick, and learned new skills, adopted new practices, and praxised your way through this book seeking transformation. You have done a magnificent job. i am so, so proud of you.

On the following pages, i want to gift you two things to help round out your journey so you may feel complete. The first is a tool: Radical Personal Alchemy. The second is a map. One thing i feel is missing in so many books on magick and personal transformation is the practical application, integration, and the embodiment of all the information—and this is where the real transformative juice lives.

III THE EMPRESS

The Tool:
Radical Personal Alchemy

What good is all the information in this book—or, indeed, in the world—if we don't know how to embody any of it in our lives? This is where Radical Personal Alchemy (RPA) comes in.

Radical Personal Alchemy encourages us to own our experiences so we may transmute them into our personal power. To understand this process better let's take a brief look at what alchemy is.

Alchemy is commonly known as the process of turning metals into gold. But it's so much more than just chemistry. Alchemy (The Great Work) is all the transformation, rituals, and self-governance we do daily, to transmute the raw materials of life (prima materia) into the substance that keeps life meaningful (The Philosopher's Stone).

Alchemy is not an end game; it's a holistic process. We do alchemy all the time without knowing it. When we take what we've learned and apply it, that's alchemy. When we create a song, lyric, poem, or letter to help process our feelings, that's alchemy. When we understand how we've hurt someone, say we're sorry, and mean it, that's alchemy. When we do our own congruency work and live our learnings, that's alchemy.

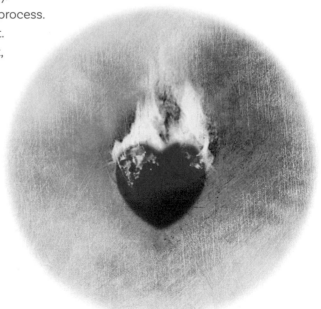

LEAP

To ground Radical Personal Alchemy into something we can work with and practice, i've unpacked the concept into four key elements: Learn. Alchemize. Express. Praxis. (L.E.A.P.) Here's how the four elements of LEAP apply to the magick for transformation journey you've been on throughout this book:

Learn: From new information (like Wild Dreams) to reframes of previously held concepts (like tarot and grimoires), you have learned so much in this book—which means you've already completed this step.

Express: Express yourself—and everything you've learned—in your own unique way. Share your experiences and help teach and transform others. This is what i hope you will do after you finish this book.

Alchemize: Brew your experiences—along with all the unique cosmology that makes you, you—and integrate them into your life. You are currently in this step now.

Praxis: Apply your unique blend to your actions and behaviors. This is what the 30-Day Challenge on the following pages will help you do.

Do you see how these four elements work together to create a complete alchemical experience? And surprise! You've actually been practicing Radical Personal Alchemy the entire time you've been reading this book!

Please know that the order of these elements can and does change. For instance, sometimes we need to first express and expel all our crap before we can learn anything new. Sometimes we need to alchemize what's already happened and learn what worked and didn't work before we can praxis and/or express ourselves differently. The order doesn't matter; making sure we include and hit every element does.

You can apply these elements to any aspect of your life—your Wild Dreams, anything you want to create, any new skill you want to learn. All impossible things can become possible through the four elements of Radical Personal Alchemy. On the following pages, we move into the praxis element of Radical Personal Alchemy by having you step into the changemaker, leader, and Firestarter you were born to be.

The Map: 30 Days of Magick for Transformation

i want nothing more than for you to live outrageously, boldly, and wildly. i desperately want you to succeed— in this and everything else you do. i've shared with you everything i know about using magick to transform your life. The rest—the application, the living of it, the actual putting it into praxis—is entirely up to you.

Like everything else in this book, i want this process to be as easy and accessible for you as possible.

To help ensure your success, i have designed a 30-day challenge to help you make the embodiment of this book a no-brainer. Just grab your grimoire, follow the daily prompts, and watch your life transform in front of you like magick. Pick a start date—today!—and begin.

Your Wild Dream Life Challenge

The following pages are intended to help you solidify your commitment to your highest self and your Wild Dream Life by guiding you through 30 days of living and praxising all the elements of this book. i've called it a challenge, because it is.

   With that said, i want you to stretch—not push yourself. That means finding a balance and rhythm that feels good to you. That may or may not look like the one i designed for you. If you feel you need more time for a particular praxis, give yourself the grace of space. The goal isn't to get it ALL in, but to take consistent, conscious action of leading yourself for 30 days straight. You can always start again, complete what you didn't finish, or do a different praxis. Just be consistent.

PRAXIS: 30-DAY CHALLENGE

DAY 0:

Read Self-leadership (see page 84) and carry out the praxis. Decide to lead yourself through the entirety of this challenge.

DAY 1:

Read Intention (see page 56). Set yours for this 30-day challenge.

DAY 2:

Read What are Wild Dreams (see page 36), and if you haven't already created My Proof List, do it today! Keep your list handy as inspiration and encouragement for the duration of the challenge.

DAY 3:

Read Belief (see page 59) and create your own mantras. Repeat these statements anytime you need a boost. Complete the "What do i believe?" praxis to ensure your beliefs are still supporting your quest for magick, and adjust as needed.

DAY 4:

Read Grimoire (see page 89). Decide how your grimoire can best support you in this challenge.

DAY 5:

Read Ancestors and Animal Allies (see page 110). Call in your allies and build your pantheon by doing the praxis. Ask your allies for their continued support in this challenge and to pave your way with omens and signs.

DAY 6:

Integration Day. Use this day to reflect on and integrate what you learned in the past five days and take one action in the spirit of it. For example, if you learned you loved setting an intention, try setting one throughout your day—before you eat, before you make a phone call, send an email, and so on. If you learned you love using your grimoire to support you, you could play with how it could support you daily.

DAY 7:

Rest and Receive Day. Use this day to stay open to what Spirit has to say. Jot down any downloads you receive. Do what you need to do to prepare for a new week of your 30-day challenge.

DAY 8:

Read What is Magick (see page 25) and do the self-assessment on page 45. Keep the Seven Hermetic Principles (see page 80) handy so you can track how well you are living them through the rest of this challenge.

DAY 9:

Read Your Wild Dream Life (see page 37), and if you haven't already created your Index Card of Wild Dreams, do it today! Keep it handy for the duration of this challenge.

DAY 10:

Read Mindset (see page 62) and do the EFT (Tapping) praxis (see page 65). This is Day One of a week of Tapping. Re-read your Index Card of Wild Dreams.

DAY 11:

Read Congruency (see page 78) and do the Seven Hermetic Principles praxis (see page 82). This is Day One of your week with the first Hermetic Principle you chose. Re-read your Index Card of Wild Dreams. For Day Two of your week of Tapping, do a round (or more!) of Tapping.

DAY 12:

Read Energy (see page 51) and follow the praxis Body Energy Centers (see page 55). Re-read your Index Card of Wild Dreams. For Day Three of your week of Tapping, do a round (or more!) of Tapping. This is Day Two of your week with the first Hermetic Principle you chose.

DAY 13:

Integration Day. Use this day to reflect on and integrate what you learned in the past five days and take one action in the spirit of it. Re-read your Index Card of Wild Dreams. For Day Four of your week of Tapping, do a round (or more!) of Tapping. This is Day Three of your week with the first Hermetic Principle you chose.

DAY 14:

Rest and Receive Day. Use this day to stay open to what Spirit has to say. Jot down any downloads you receive. Do what you need to do to prepare for a new week of your 30-day challenge. Re-read your Index Card of Wild Dreams. For Day Five of your week of Tapping, do a round (or more!) of Tapping. This is Day Four of your week with the first Hermetic Principle you chose.

DAY 15:

Half-Way Point. Read Magick, Transformation, and You (see page 32), and if you haven't already, follow the praxis to find Your Archetype Card. Keep your archetype front and center as you move through the final half of this challenge. Re-read your Index Card of Wild Dreams. For Day Six of your week of Tapping, do a round (or more!) of Tapping. This is Day Five of your week with the first Hermetic Principle you chose.

DAY 16:

Read Wild Dreams and You (see page 34) and recommit to yourself, your transformational journey, and this challenge by signing your name if you haven't already. Re-read your Index Card of Wild Dreams. For Day Seven of your week of Tapping, do a round (or more!) of Tapping. This is Day Six of your week with the first Hermetic Principle you chose.

DAY 17:

Read Sensing (see page 71) and strengthen your clair senses by following the praxis. Re-read your Index Card of Wild Dreams. This is Day Seven of your week with the first Hermetic Principle you chose.

DAY 18:

Read Intersectional Alchemy (see page 93) and follow the Web of Intersections praxis (see page 96). Re-read your Index Card of Wild Dreams. Choose another Hermetic Principle (see page 80) to spend the week with—this is Day One. Strengthen your clair senses with the Sensing praxis (see page 73).

DAY 19:

Read Medicine Wheel (see page 98) and begin the Season of the Wheel praxis (see page 101). Re-read your Index Card of Wild Dreams. This is Day Two of your week with the second Hermetic Principle you chose. Strengthen your clair senses with the Sensing praxis (see page 73).

DAY 20:

Integration Day. Use this day to reflect on and integrate what you learned in the past five days and take one action in the spirit of it. Re-read your Index Card of Wild Dreams. This is Day Three of your week with the second Hermetic Principle you chose. Strengthen your clair senses with the Sensing praxis (see page 73).

DAY 21:

Rest and Receive Day. Use this day to stay open to what Spirit has to say. Jot down any downloads you receive. Do what you need to do to prepare for a new week of your 30-day challenge. Re-read your Index Card of Wild Dreams. This is Day Four of your week with the second Hermetic Principle you chose. Strengthen your clair senses with the Sensing praxis (see page 73).

DAY 22:

Read Spiritual Will (see page 75) and do the Follow Through praxis (see page 76) for the remainder of your challenge. Re-read your Index Card of Wild Dreams. This is Day Five of your week with the second Hermetic Principle you chose. Strengthen your clair senses with the Sensing praxis (see page 73).

DAY 23:

Read Energy Work (see page 106) and Call Back Your Power with the praxis (see page 108) for the remainder of your challenge. Re-read your Index Card of Wild Dreams. This is Day Six of your week with the second Hermetic Principle you chose. Strengthen your clair senses with the Sensing praxis (see page 73). Do what you say you're going to do with the Follow Through praxis (see page 76).

DAY 24:

Read Manifesting (see page 66). Re-read your Index Card of Wild Dreams. This is Day Seven of your week with the second Hermetic Principle you chose. Strengthen your clair senses with the Sensing praxis (see page 73). Do what you say you're going to do with the Follow Through praxis (see page 76). Call Back Your Power with the Energy Work praxis (see page 108).

DAY 25:

Read Tarot (see page 115) and follow the praxis to choose your deck of transformation. Re-read your Index Card of Wild Dreams. Choose another Hermetic Principle (see page 80) to spend the week with—this is Day One. Strengthen your clair senses with the Sensing praxis (see page 73). Do what you say you're going to do with the Follow Through praxis (see page 76). Call Back Your Power with the Energy Work praxis (see page 108).

DAY 26:

Read Spirit Writing (see page 119) and try the Day 1: Freewriting praxis (see page 121). Re-read your Index Card of Wild Dreams. This is Day Two of your week with the third Hermetic Principle you chose. Strengthen your clair senses with the Sensing praxis (see page 73). Do what you say you're going to do with the Follow Through praxis (see page 76). Call Back Your Power with the Energy Work praxis (see page 108).

DAY 27:

Read Moon Magick and build a deeper connection with the moon by following the praxis (see page 104).

Re-read your Index Card of Wild Dreams. This is Day Three of your week with the third Hermetic Principle you chose. Strengthen your clair senses with the Sensing praxis (see page 73). Do what you say you're going to do with the Follow Through praxis (see page 76). Call Back Your Power with the Energy Work praxis (see page 108). Try the Day 2: Automatic Writing praxis (see page 121).

DAY 28:

Read Cosmology Of You (see page 123) and create You Base-Level Chart. Print off your chart and keep it somewhere you can see it. Re-read your Index Card of Wild Dreams. This is Day Four of your week with the third Hermetic Principle you chose. Strengthen your clair senses with the Sensing praxis (see page 73). Do what you say you're going to do with the Follow Through praxis (see page 76). Call Back Your Power with the Energy Work praxis (see page 108). Try the Day 3: Channel Writing praxis (see page 122). Build a deeper connection with the moon with the moon-gazing praxis (see page 104).

DAY 29:

Integration Day. Use this day to reflect on and integrate what you learned in the past five days and take one action in the spirit of it. Re-read your Index Card of Wild Dreams. This is Day Five of your week with the third Hermetic Principle you chose. Strengthen your clair senses with the Sensing praxis (see page 73). Do what you say you're going to do with the Follow Through praxis (see page 76). Call Back Your Power with the Energy Work praxis (see page 108). Build a deeper connection with the moon with the moon-gazing praxis (see page 104).

DAY 30:

Rest and Receive Day. Use this day to stay open to what Spirit has to say. Jot down any downloads you receive. If you choose to continue the challenge beyond 30 days, do what you need to do to prepare for a new week of challenge. Re-read your Index Card of Wild Dreams. This is Day Six of your week with the third Hermetic Principle you chose. Strengthen your clair senses with the Sensing praxis (see page 73). Do what you say you're going to do with the Follow Through praxis (see page 76). Call Back Your Power with the Energy Work praxis (see page 108). Build a deeper connection with the moon with the moon-gazing praxis (see page 104).

BONUS DAY:

Read Self-leadership (see page 84). Once you've completed the 30-Day Wild Dream Life Challenge, your next act of self-leadership is to create another 30-Day challenge for yourself! This act will help you continue to lead yourself closer to all the Wild Dream and magickal places you want to go … and grow.

FURTHER STEPS:

Once you've completed the challenge, read Magick and the Self (see page 27) and complete the journal prompts again. Journal about all the ways you have shifted, grown, transformed, and changed. Continue to study the Hermetic Principles you began on Day 11 until complete. Continue to build a deeper connection with the moon with the moon-gazing praxis (see page 104) for the next 26 days.

You did it!

i'm so proud of you.

But most importantly, you should be so f-ing proud of yourself.

Conclusion: Exeō

Everything is cyclical. And by arriving here, at the end, you find yourself back at the beginning—only this time a wiser Fool than when you began, your knapsack packed with medicine, tools, and energetic resources from your last trip around the Wheel. The Wheel has turned. And so have you.

You've released the creature comforts the Four of Pentacles warned you/i/we/us about and, through the praxis in this book, you've lived and therefore written your own Wild Dream Witch origin story. You picked up mirrors, gathered tools, and made notas to create your own invocation of magick. And it's time to leap once more.

The cards you pulled, the allies you made, the magick you created, the feats you've performed, and the transformations you've undergone, will accompany and support you as you move through Medicine Wheel time and time again. My spellcast is that this tome will continue to accompany you throughout the entirety of your journey. That it continues to serve all facets of you and iterations of your magick.

Before you close this cycle, return to the self-assessment (see page 45) and go through the prompts again. What has changed? By how much? What has stayed the same? What more does it have to tell you? Return and give thanks to who that witch was then—for they are not you now.

You have grown. You have changed. You have transformed. The first porta is complete.

Thank you. Thank you. Thank you.

Glossary

As you navigate through these pages, you'll come across some peculiar spelling and capitalization. This is all intentional and on purpose. One oddity you might find is lowercase "i"s. The usage of a capital "I" denotes the importance of the writer or the person speaking over the collective "we". Using a lowercase "i" is a conscious decision to subvert colonized language and grammar. i actively and visually deviate and protest the Western illusion of separateness and do my part to help us return to a more inclusive and collective vibe and energy.

Consciously choosing to lowercase my "i"s is the same energy and reasoning behind teaching, gathering, and meeting in a circle, where we all hold the same reverence, respect, and sovereignty—no one humxn is above or centered over the other. As a writer and creative who is actively reclaiming their Indigenousness, it's imperative to me that my art and writing are congruent with my morals and values. It is all part of the potency of my magick. Other words that might be new to your orbit can be found below.

AFAB: Assigned Female At Birth

Creatrix, folxs, and humxns/humxnity: A form of spelling that avoids socially constructed, heteronormative ideas of gender and promotes a more fluid and intersectional one.

Flients: Friends and clients.

Magick: The spelling of magick (vs. magic) is an occult one, which originated with Aleister Crowley. The additional "k" at the end differentiates between the magic of stage magicians and the spiritual, transformational, and ritualized magick that Western esotericists and occultists perform. i use it here to empower the words and work in this book by invoking the magick and energy of the collective that has been using it for decades.

Mudras: A form of India's Ayurvedic healing and a branch of yoga that involves using specific hand gestures to direct energy, focus, and awareness.

Praxis: i was first introduced to this term by Brazilian author Paulo Freire (see Resources, opposite). "Praxis" is the intersection of theory and the actionizing of that theory—aka the practice of it—and i use the term "praxis" throughout the book because i want you to be an active participant in transforming your life. i want you to take all these theories, spellwork, and rituals and do them in your own life AND reflect on how you've shifted and changed—and then how your personal shifting has impacted the people and world around you. Like my lowercase "i," the term praxis keeps the collective in mind as we work on ourselves.

Qigong: A form of Chinese Medicine that uses the body, breath, meditation, and movements to optimize energy in the body.

Reiki: The Japanese energetic healing method where the practitioner focuses their energy and intention into gentle hand movements to guide the flow of their client's energy towards healing.

Tai Chi: A movement form that uses energetic intention alone with breath and specific body shapes to create, move, and harness energy.

Tejas: Texas, USA.

Resources

Bundy, Shelby and Belew, Kate, *Wild Medicine: An Illustrated Guide to the Magick of Herbs* (Spruce Books, 2023)

Freire, Paulo, *Pedagogy of the Oppressed* (Penguin Classics, 1968)

Skyy, Brandi Amara, *Healing the Loss of a Pet* (Woke Magic Press)

Skyy, Brandi Amara, *The Little Book of Drag* (CICO Books, 2022)

Skyy, Brandi Amara, *Be More Drag* (CICO Books, 2023)

Doyle, Glennon, We Can Do Hard Things
wecandohardthingspodcast.com

Shapiro, Dani, Writing for Inner Calm: A Mindset, Methods, and Daily Exercises
skillshare.com

Skyy, Brandi Amara, The Art, Love, & Woke Magic Podcast
You can listen to the Spirit Writing episode (see page 120) of my Wild Dreams Podcast here:
brandiamaraskyy.com/art-love-and-woke-magic-podcast

Chani (moon phases app)
app.chani.com

Time Passages (moon phases app)
astrograph.com/mobile

Extra Sense (sensing app)
extrasense.en.aptoide.com/app

Bonus Material

For the free workbook and video tutorial to create the Cosmology of You chart (see page 124), EFT (tapping) videos (see page 65), examples from my own grimoire of strengthening clair senses (see page 73), and a free guide exploring how i use Intersectional Alchemy (see page 96) in my magick and how to incorporate it yourself, visit the following link:

brandiamaraskyy.com/magickfortransformation

In my tiny book, *Manifest*, i share individual praxises for each of the nine steps of manifestation. Each praxis is designed to help you understand and embody the Nine Pillars of Manifesting even more fully. You can download it for free here:

brandiamaraskyy.com/manifest-free-book

Index

Acknowledgments

There is so much magick that goes on behind the scenes of any book creation process. These are the wizards, warlocks, witches, and muggle folxs who helped manifest this book into being:

My ancestors, native lands, and Great Spirit for gifting me the spirit of this book, the medicine of every concept and idea, and permission to write it; Carmel Edmonds, my publishing editor, for taking this leap of faith with me—both the book and my capitalization and spelling requests; Kristy Richardson for editing with the same care i stitched into each and every word; Kate Belew for lending your magick and poet heart to help cast this book as a spell with your foreword; Dana Barber for being the first person (outside my parents and wife) to believe in me—and backing that belief with unwavering support; My former graduate professor and thesis advisor turned astro BFF, AnaLouise Keating, for your suggestions on the parts i was most afraid of sharing; My parents for always checking in and making sure i was writing; My wife for continuing to be one the biggest reasons why i write; And June, for always offering up her belly to be rubbed when she saw i was working too hard and needed a break.

Mucho mas love and wild magick to you all. Thank you. Thank you. Thank you.

Picture Credits

Key: t = top; c = center; b = bottom; l = left; r = right

Illustrations © CICO Books
All illustrations by **Victoria Fomina** except for the following:
Sarah Perkins: pages 1, 14, 15, 27, 30, 32, 41, 43, 60br, 75, 76bl, 77br, 85b, 92l, 96tr, 122bl, 125, 129, 130; **Melissa Launay:** pages 10t, 17t, 18, 24, 28, 33br, 36, 46, 50, 58bl, 88, 97bc, 116, 118b, 128bl; **Dionne Kitching:** pages 16, 51, 56–57, 95, 112tr, 113b; **Rohan Daniel Eason:** pages 19t, 115; **Amy-Louise Evans:** pages 21, 34b, 131; **Emma Garner:** pages 25, 54tr, 96bl, 109t, 114b; **Clare Nicholas:** pages 31br, 38cr, 59, 62, 63, 64br, 67br, 72, 73br, 74br, 100cr, 119; **Barbara Tamilin:** pages 47br, 78, 89, 91br, 100br, 123.
Tarot cards on pages 17, 24, 33, 50, 88, 97, 116, and 128 taken from *The Golden Tarot* by Liz Dean, published by CICO Books. Tarot cards on pages 19 and 115 taken from *The Elemental Power Tarot* by Melinda Lee Holm, published by CICO Books.

Illustrations © AdobeStock
Livinskiy: textured backgrounds on pages 1, 3, 5, 6–7, 12–13, 14, 17, 18–19, 21, 26–27, 29, 31, 33, 35, 37, 39, 45, 47, 52–53, 57, 58, 60, 62, 67, 68, 70, 73, 74, 80–81, 82, 85, 90, 92, 94, 96, 100, 107, 111, 120, 130; **Little Monster 2070:** stars on pages 3, 6, 26, 29, 35, 37, 52, 68, 78, 90, 107, 120, 123; **JeromeCronenberger:** page 55br; **anitapol:** page 92tl